FURNISHING THE
OLD-FASHIONED GARDEN

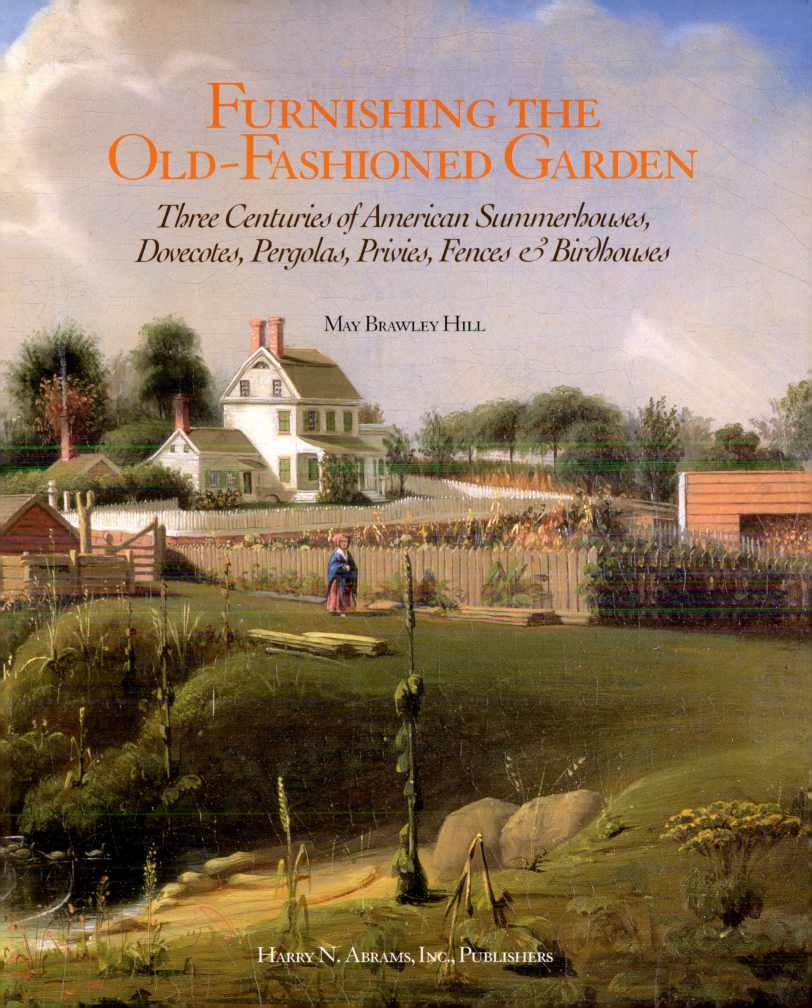

Furnishing the Old-Fashioned Garden

Three Centuries of American Summerhouses, Dovecotes, Pergolas, Privies, Fences & Birdhouses

May Brawley Hill

Harry N. Abrams, Inc., Publishers

For B.

"So many of my garden blessings have flowed from the same source that I should like well to make acknowl-
edgment here to the great and generous gardener to whom I owe so much but I dare not mention his name
lest I bring down upon him a horde of eager Cowslip lovers, and thus forever disrupt his peace and quiet."
LOUISE BEEBE WILDER, ADVENTURES IN MY GARDEN AND ROCK GARDEN (1923)

Editor: RUTH A. PELTASON
Designer: ANA ROGERS
Rights and Reproductions: LAUREN BOUCHER

PAGE 1: Charles Francis Saunders and his wife under the arbor at 580 North Lake Road, Pasadena.
Photograph, c. 1900. The Huntington Library, San Marino, California
Nature writer Charles Francis Saunders was influenced by Mission gardens when he came to make his own at the turn of the century. Laid out in terraces
rather than within a patio, the garden was backed by a grape arbor and enclosed in a latticed redwood fence covered with Cherokee and Banksia roses.

PAGES 2–3: W. R. Hamilton (c. 1810–1866). LANDSCAPE VIEW OF A HOUSE AND GARDEN. 1836. Oil on canvas, 17½ x 23½ in. Private collection
The garden of this white house was enclosed in a white picket fence and its vegetable plot in unpainted planks.

Library of Congress Cataloging-in-Publication Data

Hill, May Brawley.
Furnishing the old-fashioned garden : three centuries of American summerhouses,
dovecotes, privies, pergolas, fences, and birdhouses / May Brawley Hill.
p. cm.
Includes bibliographical references (p.   ) and index.
ISBN 0–8109–3335–7 (hardcover)
1. Garden structures—United States. 2. Garden ornaments and furniture—United States.
I. Title
NA8450.H55 1998
717'.0973—dc21   98–6422

Text copyright © 1998 May Brawley Hill
Illustrations copyright © 1998 Harry N. Abrams, Inc.
Published in 1998 by Harry N. Abrams, Incorporated, New York
All rights reserved. No part of the contents of this book may be reproduced
without the written permission of the publisher

Printed and bound in Hong Kong

Harry N. Abrams, Inc.
100 Fifth Avenue
New York, N.Y. 10011
www.abramsbooks.com

CONTENTS

Pauline Palmer (1867–1938). FROM MY STUDIO WINDOW. 1907. Oil on canvas, 31 x 25 in. Union League Club of Chicago
*Pauline Palmer's studio was in the Tree Building in Chicago, although she spent summers
in Provincetown, Massachusetts, where this picket-fenced garden may have been painted.*

INTRODUCTION

Americans will habitually prefer the useful to the beautiful,
and they will require that the beautiful be useful.
ALEXIS DE TOCQUEVILLE, DEMOCRACY IN AMERICA, 1840

As AMERICANS, WE HAVE LONG HAD A SENSE of our culture as distinct from that of any country that has contributed to our diverse population. For our home grounds we have appropriated plants and garden architecture from all over the world, but the gardens of which they are a part and the uses made of them—the inflection, as it were—have been American ones. Writers have tried to define this quality with nouns such as informality, practicality, individuality, ingenuity, and the like. De Tocqueville, for example, observed that Americans prefer the useful to the beautiful. Even so great an aesthete as Thomas Jefferson was as obsessed with the function of the many garden buildings he designed as with their appearance. Nonetheless, over the past three hundred years, Americans have found in their home gardens space to demonstrate both their desire for beauty and for imaginative flights of architectural fancy in even the most utilitarian of objects, resulting in a wealth of appealing structures.

This sampling of the alluring architectural elements found in American gardens grew from my own gardening experiences, as did my previous book, *Grandmother's Garden* (1995). Before writing it, I had collected American gardening literature in search of a garden appropriate to our eighteenth-century Connecticut farmhouse. There I read of the old-fashioned garden, or "grandmother's garden," a traditional American cottage garden of familiar perennials and native plants. Over the last five years, as my own old-fashioned garden took shape, I began to research appropriate structures and fencing to give its informally planted beds an architectural anchor. While many books on garden decoration have been published recently, none have concentrated on the tradition of such structures in American gardens, nor have they located individual trellises, arbors, fences, summerhouses, and other outbuildings in the context of specific period, place, and garden style.

My curiosity was aroused. I wanted to know when the hexagonal, bell-roofed summerhouse, often used today, first appeared in this country and what "necessaries," so frequently mentioned in early garden descriptions, looked like. I wondered what role dovecotes had played in the garden, and if they were still being made. I asked myself why the pergola had become so widespread around 1900, and what its sudden popularity revealed about American life. And specifically, I wanted to know what sort of structures would fit into the context of a weathered clapboard house, or an adobe ranch, or a bungalow, or a modern split-level. I was eager to know what the latest fashions in garden furnishings were when these houses were first built.

In my pursuit of garden structures, I looked for evidence of their use, as well as their appearance. American paintings, period photographs, historical narratives, and personal recollections offered a wealth of information and fascinating individual stories. Local collections of photographs, such as those in the Houston Public Library, the San Francisco Public Library, and the Society for the Preservation of New England Antiquities, among thousands of others across the country, contain overwhelming visual riches just beginning to be mined by garden historians.

The nomenclature of American garden architecture is often telling in itself. In the eighteenth century, the smokehouse, well house, or springhouse revealed their function in their names if not always in their appearance. *Necessary house* was the euphemism for the indispensable privy, often made a decorative garden feature. The term *greenhouse,* used in the eighteenth century for what is now called an orangery, meant a building with large windows on its south side for over-wintering tender plants. In the mid-nineteenth century, the "picturesque" garden and a passion for rustic garden structures evidenced the persuasive publications of Andrew Jackson Downing. The use of *pergola* for an arbor revealed the pervasive influence of the Arts and Crafts movement in the decades around 1900, as well as the growing sophistication of home gardeners.

An evolving garden vocabulary, accompanying changes in the garden's layout and use, gained broad currency from the proliferation of publications devoted to gardening and the home. Americans have long depended on the written word for self-education; how-to books on all aspects of life and culture have been available since early in the country's history. A succession of general trends in styles of layout, planting, and garden structures can be traced through house pattern books, gardening books and magazines, and general-interest publications. Even so, the often contradictory and even contentious advice given in an ever-increasing number of publications meant that many home gardeners did what their parents had done, followed the example of their neighbors, or did just what they wanted, unaffected by the latest style. American gardeners have shown a willingness to try almost anything in any combination, and if it works to use it. Notions of the stylish or tasteful have never limited American ingenuity.

In this very personal tour through three centuries of American garden history, I have focused on handcrafted wooden garden structures, less ephemeral than plants, and occasionally still in their original positions. The choice of possibilities was vast, and my selections are undoubtedly as idiosyncratic as are some of the structures. I was drawn particularly to those that seemed to embody some telling aspect of our American gardening experience, structures often as relevant today as when they were made.

The garden structures that characterize an era, their location and function, can reveal much about values and ways of life, as well as changes in architectural style and garden design. Gardening as recreation rather than as a necessity has historically been the avocation of the wealthy and literate. In eighteenth-century America, the increasing affluence of farmers, craftsmen, and merchants and the spread of literacy meant that members of the middle class in increasing numbers began to garden for pleasure. While the gardens of northern nabobs and southern planters of this era are well documented and have been the subjects of many published studies, more modest pleasure gardens of the same time have left fewer traces and are consequently little known. Though unpretentious and small in scale, those for which there is some evidence lack neither historical interest nor aesthetic merit.

By the nineteenth century, pleasure gardening had blossomed into a popular pastime. Nurseries sprang up everywhere, horticultural societies and garden clubs abounded, books and magazines devoted to instructing American gardeners were published by the score. Horticultural societies led by New York (1818), Pennsylvania (1827), and Massachusetts (1829) spread across the country. By the end of the century, gardening ideas and plant discoveries from all over the world were disclosed to American home gardeners in popular magazines as well as in specialized horticultural ones.

The gardens made by these unassuming gardeners are less difficult to document than those of the colonial era—there are many more of them, some of outstanding merit. Although they are little known in comparison to the great estates of the same time, these gardens form part of our astonishingly diverse vernacular garden heritage. They have given innumerable twentieth-century gardeners roots in the past and inspiration for the present. Today, as never before, we mine our history for meaningful objects for our gardens even as the startling innovations of contemporary landscape designers propel the American garden into the twenty-first century.

I know nothing so charming as our own country. The learned say it is a new creation; and I believe them; not for their reasons, but because it is made on an improved plan. Europe is a first idea, a crude production, before the maker knew his trade, or had made up his mind as to what he wanted.

THOMAS JEFFERSON, LETTER TO ANGELICA CHURCH, 1788

Ornaments *and* Necessities *in* Colonial Gardens

THE FIRST NECESSITY IN EARLY AMERICAN gardens was a fence to keep out roaming livestock. Wood, available in abundance, was used for plank, paling, picket, or other board fences with utility rather than beauty the object. The earliest gardens combined vegetables and herbs with flowers and fruit trees, but by the mid-eighteenth century a separate pleasure garden for flowers could be found on country estates and substantial town lots North and South. Enclosed flower gardens near the house were laid out symmetrically with geometric beds flanking a central path and flowering shrubs and small trees around the perimeter.

On large properties, the house was often sited to take advantage of a prospect over the countryside. A slope behind or before the house was usually terraced and bisected by a central pathway with steps between each terrace. The area immediately in front of the house was sometimes enclosed as a forecourt, with the flower garden in the back or off to one side. On small properties, the forecourt often became the enclosed dooryard flower garden, with utilitarian structures located in the yard between house and barn.

Before the Revolution, gardening was viewed as a suitable recreation for gentlemen, whether wealthy or only comfortably established. For these classically educated amateurs, a garden was not just an attractive place to walk through and admire, but an experience meant to stir a visitor's mind and imagination. The cultural associations of a garden as well as its aesthetic appeal were highly prized. Columned garden structures evoked the heroic classical past. Copies of antique sculpture or busts of historical figures terminating walks or centering beds offered evidence of the proprietor's taste, often his political views, as well as his status.

Anonymous. FRIENDS ALMSHOUSE, WALNUT STREET, PHILADELPHIA. c. 1848.
Oil on canvas, 18 x 24¾ in. Schwarz Gallery, Philadelphia
The garden of the almshouse, founded in 1713, was entered through an archway from the street.
Here the residents grew vegetables, and perhaps flowers as well, to contribute to their support.

VIEW OF THE SEAT OF THE HON. MOSES GILL, ESQ. AT PRINCETON, IN THE COUNTY OF WORCESTER, MASSA'TS. Engraving by Samuel Hill in *Massachusetts Magazine* 4 (November 1792). Boston Athenaeum

Gill's forecourt, ornamented with two statues, seen at rear center, was defined by an elegant fence of Chinese fretwork panels topped with finials. The flower garden, off to one side, was laid out in rectangular beds punctuated with small trees. A latticework summerhouse terminated the central path.

FENCES

Fences around these pleasure gardens could be quite elegant and presented a marked contrast to the more utilitarian ones enclosing the yard, vegetable garden, or pastures. Moses Gill's farm in Princeton, Massachusetts, settled in the 1760s, for example, was noted in a 1793 history of Worcester County as having "very elegant fences."[1] The Chinese railings between the ball-topped posts that defined the forecourt of his house were certainly unusual, but designs for such fretwork could be found in William Halfpenny's *Rural Architecture in the Chinese Taste* (1755), among other English pattern books. Gill's yard and orchard were surrounded by an ordinary picket fence, and his pastures by stone walls.

In the South, brick walls were used by wealthy gardeners to enclose both kitchen and flower gardens as at George Washington's "Mount Vernon" near Alexandria, Virginia. Ordinary rail fences, usually confined to fields, could

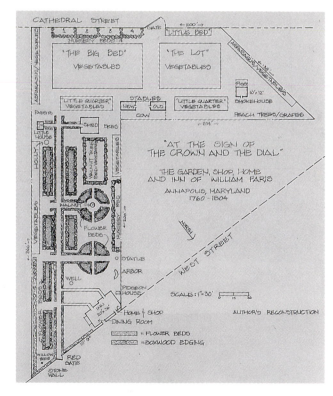

be used with dramatic effect on smaller properties, as they were by Dr. Henry Stevenson of Baltimore in the 1760s. The entrance drive to his house bisected a series of five grass terraces and was lined with a rail fence backed with trees that exaggerated the length of the approach. His formal four-bed parterre was located on the opposite side of the house.[2]

More modest pleasure gardens usually had paling or picket fences, such as clockmaker William Faris's miniature flower parterres in Annapolis, Maryland. Beginning in the 1760s, Faris laid out geometric beds and boxwood-bordered paths behind his house and shop, enclosing them with a picket fence and stone wall. He filled his flower beds with thousands of wildly popular tulips and developed several new varieties himself. He named two of these 'Cincinnatus' and 'Cato' after Roman notables, and others for American political and military figures.

Paths were grass except the stone-and-shell main path that led from Faris's red-painted front gate through the property to the vegetable garden, stables, and smokehouse at the back. At the path's end, the privy to one side was balanced by a garden shed on the other. Faris made a focal point of his necessary house, which he called his "temple," and surrounded the wooden privy with boxwood-bordered flower beds. It is noteworthy that Faris also included a statue in his pleasure garden, an indication that he was as much concerned with the garden's cultural meaning as were more highly placed gardeners. Among other more useful ornaments were an arbor planted with scarlet runner beans, beehives, and a wooden pigeon house.[3]

DOVECOTES Dovecotes had been an early feature of southern gardens, providing a supply of tasty birds as well as decorative structures. At "Shirley" on the James River in Virginia, a circular brick dovecote with a conical roof existed as early as 1686.[4] Similar dovecotes with conical roofs embellished gardens on eighteenth-century plantations such as "Parlange," in New Roads, Louisiana, where the original twin hexagonal ones still flank the entrance drive.

Such outbuildings were a necessity to house all the animals and activities on a self-sufficient farm or plantation. A smokehouse, springhouse, wagon or carriage house, woodshed, corncrib, dairy house, and poultry and pig houses were usually located in the yard between the farmhouse and barn on small holdings. On larger estates, a particularly decorative dovecote or springhouse was often made a feature of the pleasure garden. One of Thomas Jefferson's more fanciful unbuilt designs for "Monticello" in Charlottesville, Virginia, was a dovecote to be incorporated into the roof of a classical temple drawn from a plate in English architect William Gibbs's *Book of Architecture* (1728).

ARBORS   Among the earliest structures in many colonial gardens were grape arbors. In his journal of 1629, the Rev. Francis Higginson mentioned the Salem, Massachusetts, vineyard cultivated with success by Governor John Endicott. By the eighteenth century, arbors were being used decoratively to separate areas of the

Joseph Ropes (1812–1885). HOUSE OF ISAAC BLISS, HARTFORD, CONNECTICUT. 1854. Oil on canvas, 20½ x 26 in. Connecticut Historical Society, Hartford
This c. 1730 saltbox had an office flanking the central path to the front door and garden to the side, all enclosed in a plank fence.

Reuben Moulthrop (1763–1814). MRS. DANIEL TRUMAN AND CHILD. C. 1800.
Oil on canvas, 38¾ x 37¼ in. The New-York Historical Society, New York
*In New England, the enclosed dooryard or forecourt with its central walk lingered
well into the nineteenth century.*

English copperplate-printed
linen fabric. 1760–80 (detail).
Courtesy Winterthur Museum,
Delaware
*Such fabrics, printed with
figures and fanciful structures,
often Chinese, were used for bed
hangings and quilts.*

pleasure garden or to divide the flower beds from the vegetable garden and orchard. In
the John Cotton Smith garden in Sharon, Connecticut, begun in the 1770s, a long arbor,
bisected by the main path from the house, screened the vegetable beds.[5] More formally,
the grape arbor in the Benjamin Waller garden in Williamsburg, Virginia, covered a
path crossing the main one, the juncture marked by an open-sided garden pavilion.

Plain wooden arches, like those forming grape arbors, occasionally marked divi-
sions in the garden, as they did at Elias Hasket Derby's farm in Danvers, Massachusetts.
Here, single white-painted arches with keystones spanned the steps that separated the
three garden terraces enclosed in a slat fence. Indefatigable garden visitor clergyman
William Bentley, who described the garden on a visit in 1790, also noted the "superb
fence" around the house.[6] (Similar arches remain in the Pierce-Nichols garden, Salem,
Massachusetts, dating to the 1790s.)

Eighteenth-century taste preferred green-painted arbors. Publications such as

Thomas Dobson's *Encyclopedia or Dictionary of Arts and Science* (Philadelphia, 1798) gave instructions for mixing the necessary green paint using verdigris, white lead, and linseed oil, and noted, "the green is of great service in the country for doors, window shutters, arbours, garden seats, rails . . . ."[7]

BENCHES AND SEATS

Thomas Jefferson designed a bench with a three-section Chinese fretwork back and poplar seat for his terraces at "Monticello" and specified that it be painted green. A similar garden bench of yellow pine, with a four-section slat back, was used at "Almodington" in Somerset County, Maryland. The original color of this bench was white. While these benches were made at home, craftsmen were available to make garden furniture to order. One of these advertised "Garden Seats, made and painted to particular directions," in the *Baltimore Daily Repository* in 1791.[8]

The Andrews house, Bethel, Connecticut. Photograph, c. 1865. Collection Schrijver family
Although taken in the 1860s, this photograph shows a rural New England homestead little changed from the previous century. The modest grape arbor sheltering beehives separated the house dooryard from the barnyard, while a stone wall fronted the road.

Windsor chairs and benches, introduced early in the eighteenth century, were used outside as well as indoors; drawings of the time show them on porches and in gardens North and South. In 1765, a New York craftsman offered for sale such chairs "fit for Piazza or Gardens."[9] By 1800, there were several dozen Windsors on the piazza of George Washington's "Mount Vernon" offering accommodation to the hordes of visitors there.

SUMMERHOUSES Robert Beverly observed in his *History and Present State of Virginia* (1705) that the "Inconvenience" of oppressive summer heat "is made easie by cool Shades, by open Airy rooms, Summer-Houses, Arbors, and Grottos." He enjoyed, in his father-in-law William Byrd's garden, "a Summer-House set round with Indian Honey-Suckle, which all the Summer is continually full of sweet Flowers . . . ."[10] Such summerhouses, or garden houses, became ubiquitous on both large and small properties and were usually the focal point of their gardens. At the Moravian settlement Bethabara in the North Carolina piedmont, the communal vegetable garden, known from a plan of 1759, was surrounded by a picket fence and divided into nine

square beds. An arched grape arbor separated two of the beds and terminated in a summerhouse surrounded with clove pinks, daffodils, and lilacs. The adjacent garden for
medicinal plants was centered on another summerhouse, and there was yet another
perched on an island in the stream that bordered the settlement.[11]

On large estates, garden houses were often classical in inspiration if not literal
copies of buildings reproduced in the many drawing books by English architects such as
William Kent and James Gibbs. For example, in South Carolina while visiting Alexander Middleton's "Crowfield" in the 1740s, Eliza Lucas discovered with delight "a large
fish pond with a mount . . . and upon it . . . a roman temple." [12]

From the more imposing summerhouses, a visitor could have a prospect of the
entire garden. Isaac Royall's summerhouse in Medford, Massachusetts, dating to midcentury, stood on a mound at the terminus of the path through the garden from the house.
Also around this time, the octagonal garden house crowned with an outsized cupola at
"Montpelier Manor" near Laurel, Maryland, was the terminus of a box-bordered avenue,
the cross axis of the formal garden. A stone structure of similar form, but with a concave

pagoda roof rather than a bell-shaped one, served as a bathhouse at "Trentham" near Baltimore and was furnished with two mahogany tubs.[13] Springhouses or bathhouses, as cooling in the summer as a grotto, could occupy the position of a garden pavilion, and large estates North and South often had both.

Not all such structures were tethered to the ground. Mrs. Anne Grant in her *Memoirs of an American Lady* (1808) recalled a visit in 1763 to the British fort at Oswego, New York, where the commander had made a garden containing "a summer house in a tree . . . ."[14]

CHINESE TASTE Master carpenters were available to construct elaborate fences, arbors, and summerhouses. One carpenter advertised in the *Virginia Gazette* in 1774 that he could build "all sorts of *Chinese* and *Gothick* PALING for gardens and summer houses."[15] The opening of China to trade with the West, and the resulting influx of goods and textiles, including painted wallpapers, resulted in a taste for chinoiserie in gardens as well as for interior decoration. The sprightly concave roof that began to appear on garden buildings was one such borrowing from China—fretwork in railings, fences, and bench backs was another.

Baroness Hyde de Neuville (c. 1779-1849). THE MOREAU HOUSE, 2 JULY, 1809. Brown wash over pencil, 7 x 12⅜ in. Courtesy Museum of Fine Arts, Boston. M. and M. Karolik Collection (58.920) *Windsor chairs furnished the porch and a statue and potted plants ornamented the enclosed front garden of this modest house in the French settlement at Morristown, New Jersey.*

Charles Willson Peale. WILLIAM PACA. 1772. Oil on mattress ticking, 88⅜ x 58¼ in. Maryland Historical Society, Baltimore

Governor William Paca's elegant octagonal two-story garden house, seen in the background of his portrait, served as the terminus to the axial path through his garden in Annapolis, Maryland.

Fanciful pavilions, whether Chinese, classical, or Gothic, had widespread currency as decorative images and could be found printed on eighteenth-century English copperplate fabrics and American wallpapers.[16] In gardens they offered an engaging alternative to classical structures. Thomas Handasyd Perkins, who had made a fortune in the Chinese opium trade, went so far as to have a poultry house built in the form of a Chinese pagoda on his estate "Pinebank" in Brookline, Massachusetts.[17]

Joseph Barrell, another merchant in the China trade who introduced many plants from China into cultivation, had an elegant garden in Boston, Massachusetts. The Rev. William Bentley in 1791 marveled that "No expense is spared to render the whole amusing, instructive and friendly." Included were a pond with a marble statue in the center, dovecotes, and a flower garden divided into square parterres, each centered with sculpture. Beyond the flower garden stood an imposing two-story summerhouse in the Chinese taste, with a hothouse occupying the ground floor.[18]

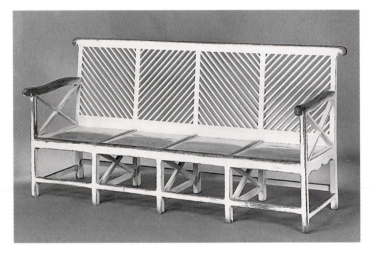

Garden seat from Somerset County, Maryland. 1780. Painted yellow pine, 96¼ x 45½ x 28 in. Museum of Early Southern Decorative Arts, Winston-Salem, North Carolina
William Halfpenny's pattern book Rural Architecture in the Chinese Taste *(London 1755) pictured a similar bench.*

"Belmont" near Philadelphia, begun in mid-century, was rich in topiary obelisks, pyramids, and balls, as well as sculptures of Fame, Mercury, and Diana, and featured a Chinese temple as a summerhouse. Deborah Logan, who herself had a notable garden at "Stenton" in Germantown, Pennsylvania, visited "Belmont" in 1819. Such formal gardens were out of fashion, to judge from her comment, "the garden is quite a curiosity from exhibiting a most perfect sample of the taste of Parterres and arbors made of Yew clipped into forms . . . ."[19]

THE NATURAL STYLE   Before the Revolution, a few landowners had been swayed by the changing English taste away from formal gardens to a more natural style in landscaping, limited to wood, water, and lawn exemplified in the grand landscapes, designed by Lancelot "Capability" Brown. Gardeners able to travel to England made a point of visiting properties laid out in the new style. Thomas Whately's *Observations on Modern Gardening* (1770), which described many of these estates, was owned by educated gardeners in America, including Thomas Jefferson, who used the book as a guide on his tour of 1786. In 1766, Richard Stockton visited Alexander Pope's garden at Twickenham, near London, and on his return to Princeton, New Jersey, made improvements to his garden at "Morven." Lord Burlington's famous gardens at Chiswick,

and poet William Shenstone's *ferme ornée,* "The Leasowes," near Hagley, were visited by Henry Lucas of Charleston, South Carolina, in the 1760s before beginning his own garden at "Mepkin" on the Cooper River. Even earlier, Eliza Lucas had visited "Crowfield" near Charleston in 1743, where she particularly enjoyed the evidences of modern taste: serpentine walks and irregular flower beds, changing perspectives and distant prospects, groves of trees and naturalistic water features.[20]

A garden in Brookline, Massachusetts, owned by Henry Hulton, Boston's commissioner of customs, seems to have been a more modest version of the natural style. As described by a visitor in the early 1770s, it had "a Large Lawn in front, Shrubs & flowers on the borders of it to imitate Nature in its Wildness & variety."[21]

Beginning in 1726, noted Virginia gardener William Byrd II made changes at his "Westover" garden that combined natural features of the landscape with garden struc-

tures. John Bartram, who visited in 1738, described "new gates, gravel Walks, hedges, and cedars finely twined and a little greenhouse . . . ." Another visitor drew a map of the garden as it was in 1783 that showed twin privies, marked "Temples of Cloacina," as focal points on either end of a graceful arc of trees pierced by an elegant wrought-iron entrance gate.[22]

PRIVIES In both modest and grand gardens, formal or informal, decorative privies, or necessary houses, made a virtue of necessity. In the North, where privies were located as close to the house as possible, often in a connected outbuilding, they were occasionally made a decorative garden feature as at the Lord House in Ipswich, Massachusetts.

Governor Spotswood's formal flower garden at Williamsburg, Virginia, begun about 1717, had featured diamond-patterned parterres with necessary houses fit into the corners of the garden wall. A similar arrangement prevailed in less pretentious southern gardens. A painting of "Holly Hill," Anne Arundel County, Maryland, shows a forecourt garden of about the same date having four square beds enclosed in a paling fence with modest necessaries fitted into the outer corners.[23] A German tourist to the Chesapeake region in 1783 remarked that even in towns, privies were outside the houses, most properties having "a little court or garden, where usually are the necessaries, and so this often evil-smelling convenience of our European houses is missed here, but space and better arrangement are gained."[24]

George Washington's "Mount Vernon" boasted perhaps the most visited necessary houses of the time. In the twinned flower and kitchen gardens, laid out in 1760 and enlarged in 1785, elegant wooden pepper pot structures are tucked into the corners nearest the house as well as into the curves of the walls at the points farthest away. Those nearest were the necessaries; the other two were reserved for storage of tools and seeds.

Although Washington never traveled to England, his design for "Mount Vernon" reflected a knowledge of current ideas about landscape gardening, including the importance of prospect and the use of curving paths and groves of trees for changing viewpoints. As was the case with so many other Americans, his ideas were formed by reading and through contact with other passionate gardeners, as well as practical experience. Throughout the colonies, a vital community of plantsmen and -women was maintained through personal visits and a vast network of correspondence. In Washington's struggles to perfect his own greenhouse in the 1780s, for example, he consulted Mrs. Charles Carroll, who had a noted one at "Mount Clare" outside Baltimore.[25]

GREENHOUSES AND FLOWERPOTS Greenhouses and
hothouses were ruinously expensive to construct and maintain and were found only in
gardens of the very wealthy and most passionate plantsmen such as William Hamilton.
The pride of his estate, "The Woodlands," outside Philadelphia, was a greenhouse flanked
by two hothouses with a combined length of 140 feet containing upward of ten thousand
plants. This was grand indeed. Washington's greenhouse, as such minimally heated
orangeries were termed in the eighteenth century, was only forty feet long. That at "Wye
House," in Tidewater Maryland, measured eighty-six feet counting both the central block
and flanking wings.[26] Even these were exceptional. Most American gardeners had to
content themselves with a sunny window and modest clay pots for any tender plants they
wanted to bring through the winter.

Before the Revolution, potteries supplying redware for the kitchen and table also
made flowerpots. Most were very simple in form, occasionally enlivened with colored
slip or an ornamental rim, and were used decoratively in both house and garden. A 1751
notice in the *New York Gazette* offered "vases, urns, flower pots, etc. to ornament gardens or the tops of houses, or any other ornament made of clay . . . ."[27]

The pottery in the Moravian village of Salem, North Carolina, settled in the
1750s, supplied flowerpots as well as essential kitchenware from its inception. As did the
lots for residences in this church-controlled village, the pottery lot had room for a garden. Here in the 1820s a visitor noted a living summerhouse made of eight cedar trees
that had been planted in a circle forty years before, the tops chained together. The resulting cone-shaped shelter was "beautifully trimmed perfectly even and very thick within,
[there] were seats placed around and doors were cut through the branches . . . ."[28]

BIRDHOUSES Potteries also furnished the nesting bottles or
"martin pots," mentioned in many eighteenth-century inventories, that were designed
to be hung in the garden or from the eaves of the house. Voracious insects, along with
extremes of temperature, have always plagued American gardeners. It was noted early
on by both naturalists and gardeners that smaller birds like flycatchers, bluebirds, mar-
tins, and wrens ate tremendous numbers of annoying insects in a day. Many ingenious
objects for their comfortable accommodation were thus devised, ranging from wooden
boxes to old hats, with convenient holes, nailed up on a tree. Mrs. Anne Grant in her
account of life in Albany, New York, before the Revolution remarked on the "unseemly
ornaments" of animal skulls nailed to fenceposts around the vegetable garden as nesting

Lord house, Ipswich, Massachusetts. Photograph, c. 1890.
Society for the Preservation of New England Antiquities, Boston

On this cramped village lot enclosed with a picket fence, palings divided the front entrance from the side yard where a lilac sheltered the privy.

sites. She described with approval the more acceptable shelf built for nests under the roof of the entrance portico of the Schuyler house, where she had been a visitor.[29]

Architectural birdhouses, usually called "wren boxes," were occasionally mentioned in late-eighteenth-century records. In 1780, a Boston painting firm charged merchant Joseph Barrell for "painting a wren box." Some, like the two painted "in imitation of North Church" and "the New Brick Meeting House" by the same firm, must have been quite impressive. Martin houses were also in use, and a diary entry from 1796 mentioned five martin houses on poles in one Maine garden.[30]

He is an American, who leaving behind him all his ancient prejudices and manners, receives new ones from the new mode of life he has embraced, the new government he obeys, and the new rank he holds. . . . The American is a new man, who acts upon new principles; he must therefore entertain new ideas, and form new opinions.

MICHEL-GUILLAUME-JEAN DE CRÈVECOEUR, LETTERS FROM AN AMERICAN FARMER, 1782

THE NEW REPUBLIC, 1780–1810

AFTER THE REVOLUTION, CITIZENS OF THE fledgling United States could no longer consider themselves English, culturally or politically. In Thomas Jefferson's inaugural address as president in 1801, he spoke of his vision of America as a revolutionary republic, "a rising nation, spread over a wide and fruitful land."[1] Indeed the nation's size would be doubled by the Louisiana Purchase of 1803 and already encompassed previously English and French holdings in the new Northwest Territory. Jefferson's vision for America even influenced the shape of the Midwest landscape through the rational geometric grid imposed on the land by the Northwest Ordinance of 1783.

Ancient Rome, rather than contemporary Britain, was the fitting model for the new republic. Writings on agriculture by Pliny the Younger, Cicero, Horace, and Virgil had led to an association of Roman virtues with pastoral life. The growing middle class as well as wealthy landowners embraced the ideal embodied in Cincinnatus, called from his plow to assume state leadership and eager to return to his farm at the end of his service. Both garden structures and newly built houses began to reflect a taste for Roman temple forms. In the garden they functioned as symbols of American independence, just as classical porticos on new houses signaled virtuous citizens within.

THE AMERICAN LANDSCAPE GARDEN In the new republic, citizens who had accumulated wealth in shipping, trade, or other professions began to acquire country properties. Only in the plantation South, as in England, was the land itself the main source of wealth and prestige. Those with new estates continued

Augustus Weidenbach (active 1850–70). BELVEDERE. c. 1858.
Oil on canvas, 34⅛ x 45³⁄₁₆ in. Maryland Historical Society, Baltimore
John Eager Howard, a governor of Maryland, was the first owner of "Belvedere," in Baltimore, completed in 1785 and noteworthy for the sculptures in its forecourt. The cast-iron seats and the evergreens, vines, and shrubs behind the curved cast-iron fence that screened the house and attached greenhouse were later additions.

to model themselves on the English landed gentry and to fashion their gardens following English precedent.

For Jefferson and other American landowners, the English eighteenth-century *ferme ornée,* with its artfully laid-out fields, orchards, ornamental kitchen gardens, and curving walks through shrubbery and flowery parterres, was an inspiration; many smaller properties North and South were described at the time using the French term.[2] Nonetheless, even those who still looked to England for guidance in gardening, as in art and literature, were influenced by the expanse and richness of the American landscape.

In many gardens made after the Revolution, the virtues of the landscapes were incorporated into the garden. At Jefferson's "Monticello," for example, an abundantly forested hill furnished the context for his improvements. As Jefferson pointed out, America "is the country of all others where the noblest gardens can be made without expense. We have only to cut out the superabundant plants."[3] Settlers moving West voiced similar sentiments. David Meade, who had left a mature garden in Williamsburg, Virginia, for a Kentucky farm, wrote enthusiastically to a friend in 1797, "there is nothing wanting but the hand of art which would form the productive farm or the delightful garden."[4]

Theodore Lyman, a Boston merchant who had prospered in the China trade, hired an English gardener to lay out the grounds of his new property in Waltham, a suburb of Boston. The New England setting of forest, hill, meadow, and stream, however, became an integral part of the landscape of "The Vale." The house, designed in 1793 by Samuel McIntire, was set in an open lawn; the stream before it widened into a serpentine canal. Behind, the forested hill was bounded by a brick wall with beds for fruit trees and flowers on its protected south face; a hothouse built into the hill was used to grow tender exotics. The grounds were ornamented with trees and shrubs, which were added to existing natives. A columned summerhouse was built into the brick wall and another summerhouse with a concave pyramidal roof formed the termination of a curving walk from the house.

Lyman's later guide to gardening was Bernard McMahon's *American Gardener's Calendar* (1806) where landscaping "in imitation of nature" was adapted to the American soil and climate. "A spacious lawn, bounded with rural shrubberies," rather than a formal parterre, was advocated by McMahon as the most suitable setting for a house, with water "in a winding course in gentle meanders" as a foreground. He advised ornamenting the pleasure grounds with "edifices such as temples, grottos, rural seats" all embowered in clumps of trees.[5]

RIGHT: Anonymous. "THE LILACS," THOMAS KIDDER RESIDENCE, FOREST STREET, MEDFORD, MASSACHUSETTS, facade. c. 1810. Watercolor on paper, 10⅜ x 16⅞ in. Society for the Preservation of New England Antiquities, Boston *The layout of the front garden, with a curved carriage drive and a circular flower bed on axis with the house entrance, appeared often on new properties large and small.*

Landscape gardens could be found in new estates in the mid-Atlantic region as well. John Penn's house outside Philadelphia was built in 1785 as a two-story cube separated from its kitchen, a smaller cube, by a circular forecourt. His garden in the natural style, known from a contemporary plan, included groves of trees threaded with paths and wilderness and flower gardens reached by a circuitous route from the house.[6]

THE SUBLIME, THE BEAUTIFUL, AND THE PICTURESQUE

At the same time that gardeners began to appropriate the particularly American landscape of forest, cleared land, mountain vistas, and broad rivers, native scenery began to assume a nationalistic importance in the minds of American writers. *The Port Folio,* a Philadelphia periodical, announced a series on American scenery in 1809 with the assertion, "our country affords an inexhaustible abundance, which for picturesque effect, cannot be surpassed in any part of the old world."[7] Washington Irving's *The Sketchbook of*

Thomas Birch (1779–1851). SOUTHEAST VIEW OF "SEDGELEY PARK," THE COUNTRY SEAT OF JAMES COWLES FISHER, ESQ. c. 1819. Oil on canvas, 34¼ x 48⅜ in. The National Museum of American Art, Smithsonian Institution, Washington, D.C. *A square summerhouse with a belfry in the Gothic style appears on the river side of the house, designed by Benjamin Latrobe in 1799.*

Anonymous. NEW ENGLAND
COUNTRY SEAT. c. 1800–22. Oil
on panel, 23 x 36⅛ in. The Art
Institute of Chicago. Gift of
Robert Allerton (1946.391)
This estate had a traditional
axial entrance and enclosed
forecourt ornamented with
conical evergreens.

Geoffrey Crayon, although written in the form of a picturesque itinerary to European
locales with historical associations, had as its premise that "never need an American look
beyond his own country for the sublime and beautiful of natural scenery."[8]

These three aesthetic terms—the beautiful, the sublime, and the picturesque—
had been central to discussions of landscape in England in the eighteenth century. English philosopher Edmund Burke had divided landscapes into those that were sublime
and evoked the emotions of awe and fear, and those that were beautiful—the Alps, for
example—versus settled, pastoral scenes. Scottish philosopher Archibald Alison proposed that an educated spectator's emotional reaction to a landscape and the objects within it were due as much to personal and historical associations with the scene as to any
qualities intrinsic to the scene. In reaction to the beautiful, if tame, landscapes created by
Lancelot Brown and his followers, essayists at the end of the century added to Burke's
two categories a third, that of the picturesque—landscapes characterized by contrasts
and irregularity, intricacy and variety. This debate was noted and the terms quickly appropriated by many literate gardeners on this side of the Atlantic.[9]

Benjamin Latrobe (1764–1820).
SKETCH OF MAJOR WATTS
LITTLE HOUSE...RICHMOND,
DRAWN FROM MEMORY,
NORFOLK MARCH 12, 1797.
Pencil, pen, and ink wash on
paper, 6⁵⁄₁₆ x 10⁵⁄₁₆ in. Maryland
Historical Society, Baltimore
*In his travels through the South,
Latrobe sketched many scenes
of daily life, including this
charming drawing of a pet
raccoon and his own little house.*

PICTURESQUE OUTBUILDINGS

Thomas Jefferson's prodigious imagination and insatiable curiosity led him to amass an impressive library, including many books on architecture. For Jefferson, and other educated citizens, Gothic as well as classical buildings were used for visual effect and for their potent associations. In 1771 he planned a Gothic temple for the family burial ground to be surrounded by "gloomy evergreens."[10] This and many other designs for garden structures were never built since Jefferson, like other American gardeners, gave priority to more util-

Summerhouse at the Hollister place, Greenfield, Massachusetts. Photograph in Charles Edward Hooper, *Reclaiming the Old House* (1913)
This simple summerhouse was supported by rustic columns with a latticework frieze.

itarian buildings. At his retreat "Poplar Forest" near Lynchburg, Virginia, begun in 1806, Jefferson flanked ornamental mounds to the east and west of the house with domed, octagonal brick privies that echoed the shape of the house. About the same time he designed a neoclassical cube with a pyramidal roof concealed behind a Chinese railing as a garden house for the retaining wall of his vegetable garden at "Monticello."[11]

Benjamin Latrobe, a British architect trained in the classical style, arrived in Virginia in 1796 and was taken under Jefferson's wing. His letters of recommendation resulted in commissions such as that from the Philadelphia merchant William Crammond in 1799 for a country place on the Schuylkill River. Latrobe's design for Crammond's house, "Sedgeley Park," grafted Gothic arched window and door openings onto a neoclassic cube, the first instance of Gothic elements used structurally in an American house.

George Francis (1790–1873). WYLLYS MANSION, HARTFORD. c. 1818. Oil on wood panel, 14⅝ x 19⅛ in. The Connecticut Historical Society, Hartford *The house, built in 1636, was sheltered by the "Charter Oak," in which Connecticut's Royal Charter was purportedly hidden in 1687. The fretwork gate and pagoda roof privy probably date to the time of Hezekiah Wyllys (1747–1827), the last family occupant.*

Latrobe was familiar with the latest ideas on landscape gardening and had little appreciation for formal parterres. When he visited Washington at "Mount Vernon" he noted in the flower garden "a parterre stripped and trimmed with infinite care into the form of a richly flourished fleur-de-lis, the expiring groan, I hope, of our grandfather's pedantry."[12] The grounds at "Sedgeley Park" were ornamented with a Gothic summer-house, curving paths, flower beds, and urns contributing to the picturesque effect.

Garden houses built in the early republic were predominantly classical in inspiration. Simple columned structures frequently formed arbors and summerhouses, as on the Hollister place in Greenfield, Massachusetts. The open-sided garden house there was once attributed to Asher Benjamin, whose first architectural book, *The Country Builder's Assistant,* was published in Greenfield in 1798.

The grand classical two-story teahouse that Samuel McIntire designed for Elias

Haskell Derby in 1794 in Peabody, Massachusetts, marked the other end of the architectural scale. Also decorating the grounds was a bark-covered hermitage sheltered by a weeping willow which, according to Eliza Southgate who visited in 1802, "bespoke the melancholy inhabitant."[13] Both classical and Gothic features occasionally appeared together in gardens, reflecting the blossoming of a romantic interest in expressive garden ornaments that would evoke emotional associations.

USEFUL AS WELL AS DECORATIVE

In 1809 James Madison added to his garden at "Montpelier," in Virginia, a circular summerhouse with freestanding Doric columns supporting a dome. Like Elias Haskell Derby's teahouse, where the ground floor was used for tool storage, the elegant "Montpelier" pavilion served a practical function—it covered an icehouse.

Anonymous. TWO CHILDREN IN AN ARBOR OF FLOWERS. c. 1820. Watercolor on paper, 20⅛ x 15¾ in. Courtesy Museum of Fine Arts, Boston. M. and M. Karolik Collection
This arbor was in Poughkeepsie, New York.

Susanna Huebner (1770–1818). HOUSE WITH SIX-BED GARDEN. 1818. Ink and watercolor on paper, 12½ x 7⅝ in. Schwenkfelder Library, Pennsburg, Pennsylvania
Susanna Huebner made this Fraktur of a dooryard garden for her nephew David.

The octagonal stone garden house at "The Highlands," in Whitemarsh, Pennsylvania, dating to the 1790s, also had a dual use—it was built over a spring with shelves for perishable foods around the walls of the lower level. Owner Anthony Morris offered "The Highlands" for sale in 1805, stressing his improvements to the place as well as its "elegant and healthy" situation and the beauty of the surrounding countryside. Morris had envisioned "The Highlands" as a *ferme ornée,* with pleasing vistas over fields from the house. In 1798 he had bought one hundred Lombardy poplars to line the curving entrance drive as well as magnolias and other ornamental trees and shrubs to surround the house. A ha-ha wall separated springhouse and lawn from pasture, and his fields were enclosed with post-and-rail fences. The vegetable garden was located out of sight at the bottom of a slope surrounded with a board fence painted white. The desire for a pleasing arrangement as well as convenience likewise dictated the placement of smokehouse, icehouse,

Well house and slave quarters, Bacon house, Woodbury,
Connecticut. Photograph in *White Pine Series of Architectural
Monographs VIII* (1922)
Four pillars support the pyramidal roof over this well.

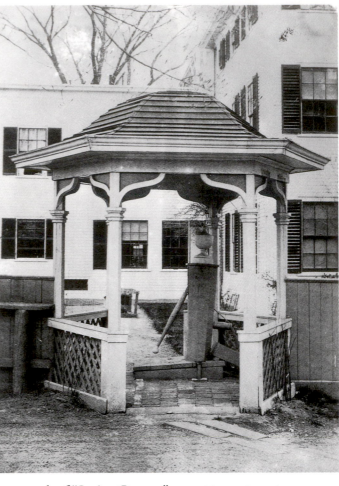

Old pump house between
Stocker-Wheelwright and
Higgins houses, 75 and 73
High Street, Newburyport,
Massachusetts. Society for the
Preservation of New England
Antiquities, Boston
*A shared well and pump became
the occasion for a hospitable
columned structure that doubled
as a summerhouse.*

and privy in an arc behind the house. The square stone
icehouse was flanked by the octagonal wood smokehouse and privy, all reached by flagstone paths.[14]

Such utilitarian buildings, often of simplified
geometrical shapes—a vernacular neoclassicism that
appealed to educated taste of the time—were frequently
used as decorative accents. A diary entry of 1788 noted
a circular icehouse with conical roof covering a spring on the grounds of "Spring Greene,"
Warwick, Rhode Island.[15] Henry Clay's house "Ashland" in Lexington, Kentucky, had
two similar icehouses, their conical roofs forming charming punctuations in the lawn to
the side of the house. At "Liberty Hall" in Union, New Jersey, occupied by the Kean family since the 1790s, spring and icehouses occupied a prominent spot at the rear of the house.

In the absence of a spring, a well was a necessity. If the well was deep enough to
require the use of pulley and rope, rather than a well sweep to dip out the water, a decorative well house was often built to house them. The resulting structure could resemble
a privy with pyramidal roof, as did that of the 1790s well house on the grounds of the
William Greene house in Warwick, Rhode Island. A similar roof supported on four
turned columns covered a well at the Rufus Barton house in Millbury, Massachusetts,
and one with plain supports protected the well at the Bacon house in Woodbury, Connecticut. Behind this Woodbury well stood slave quarters that echoed the architecture of
the clapboarded and gambrel-roofed house.[16]

THE UBIQUITOUS CUBE Square structures with pyramidal roofs, common to both northern and southern gardens, became part of the Classical Revival vernacular and were used for all sorts of outbuildings. In the garden of the Samuel Holton house in Danvers, Massachusetts, for example, a cube with a sprightly pointed roof and finial served as a two-section privy. A simpler one-room cube with pyramidal roof filled the same function on the grounds of "Plaindealing," Talbot County, Maryland.

Smokehouses, essential structures on plantations throughout the South where meat was preserved by drying rather than stored salted in barrels, were frequently built as cubes. The materials were varied: brick as at "Mt. Lebanon," Bourbon County, Kentucky; stone as at "Wheatland," Jefferson County, West Virginia; or wood as on the Kilpatrick place in Wilcox County, Alabama. Even the lowly chicken house could appear as a decorative cube as did the one topped with a diamond-shaped finial at

Privy, Samuel Holton house, Danvers, Massachusetts. Photograph by Arthur Haskell, 1933. Society for the Preservation of New England Antiquities, Boston
The summerhouse at "The Vale" was probably not dissimilar to this elegant square privy with a sprightly pagoda roof.

Smokehouse and office, "Green Plains," Mathews County, Virginia. Photograph, 1942. Collection F. H. Cabot

Charles Willson Peale. VIEW OF THE GARDEN AT BELFIELD. 1815–16. Oil on canvas, 28 x 36½ in. Private collection
Charles Willson Peale envisioned his property in Germantown as a ferme ornée in the natural style.
He ornamented the grounds near the house with the temple summerhouse that enclosed a bust of
George Washington, the greenhouse built over a spring, and the pool and fountain seen in this painting.
Other furnishings included rustic seats, an obelisk, and a Chinese summerhouse.

Anonymous. THE VALE.
1820–30. Oil on canvas, 4½ x 9½
in. Society for the Preservation
of New England Antiquities,
Boston. Gift of John Haywood
*The serpentine watercourse, the
winding paths, and the groves of
trees that were characteristic of
the natural style in landscape
gardening can be seen in this
view of "The Vale" in Waltham,
Massachusetts. The summerhouse with convex pyramidal
roof, seen on a rise to the right
of the house, no longer exists.*

"Blakely," Warren County, Mississippi. At "Ditchley" in Northumberland County, Virginia, identical wooden cubes for both icehouse and dairy flanked the brick mansion.[17]

Such balanced symmetry for outbuildings was not always the case. As Benjamin Latrobe amusingly noted in his diary, outbuildings were often clumped around southern plantations "as a litter of pigs their mother."[18]

In an alternate arrangement at "Green Plains" in Mathews County, Virginia, the outbuildings, including a carpenter's shop, weaving room, tanning house, conical icehouse, cube smokehouse, quarters, and barns, were spaced along the entrance drive. In the garden to one side of the drive, a latticed summerhouse with seats marked the crossing of two graveled paths. A notable feature of this garden of the late 1790s was the scalloped brick wall that cloistered it from the working portion of the grounds across the drive.[19]

"BELFIELD"   In 1813 painter Charles Willson Peale added to the highest point in his garden a six-column tholos, or circular temple structure, the wooden columns turned by his son Franklin. Gardening was a family affair at "Belfield," Germantown, Pennsylvania, as was the museum Peale had established in Philadelphia. Another son, Rubens, a botanist, was as involved in laying out the garden at "Belfield" as he was in running the museum.

Rubens proposed adapting as a greenhouse the arched roof springhouse that had been dug into the hillside below the house. In its new guise, it formed the focal point of Peale's circa 1815 painting of his garden with the temple visible on the left and a circular fountain, constructed the previous year, in the lower right. Rubens placed his pots of tender plants, perhaps including his precious geraniums, around the fountain's rim where, his father wrote, they made "a very handsome display."[20]

As did Thomas Jefferson, Peale felt aesthetic experiences ought to have moral consequences—instruction, as well as amusement, was the aim of both his museum and his garden. For Jefferson, meaning was implicit in the garden structures themselves. Peale, looking back to the rationalism of the previous century, made instruction explicit in his garden ornaments. A program of images and inscriptions related the structures to Peale's personal life and political beliefs.

In his autobiography, Peale gave an account of his garden as an important part of "the portrait of the man," especially "all his fripperies and follies . . . as all these things were made of wood and paint, which could last only a few years." Among these were a wooden obelisk, erected in 1813 as the terminus of a walk behind the house, whose pedestal he inscribed with aphorisms.[21] Other ornaments were a pedestal listing ninety important events in American history and a toolbox made into a garden seat decorated with figures symbolizing America and Congress. Peale inscribed the facade of his Chinese summerhouse with a text for meditation "on the past, on the present, and on the future."[22] Other rustic seats, meant solely for rest and enjoyment, were spaced along the gravel paths.

BENCHES AND SEATS Gardeners like Peale, who enjoyed designing and constructing their own garden ornaments, could have found helpful suggestions in books published in England but available here, such as C. Middleton's *Decorations for Parks and Gardens: Designs for gates, garden seats, alcoves, temples, baths, etc.* (1800). Although the rage for rustic seats and pavilions would not peak until the mid-nineteenth century, several early books included such ornaments. Charles Ober's *Ornamental Architecture in the Gothic, Chinese and Modern Taste* (1758), for example, contained many designs for garden structures to be built with tree roots.

Furniture of various sorts migrated from house to garden to supplement more permanent benches and seats. The campeachy chair, a comfortable lounger of wood with leather upholstery, occasionally joined the Windsor and locally made slat-back chairs for outdoor seating. An 1819 drawing by Latrobe shows a campeachy in use on a terrace in

New Orleans. The name of the chair, as well as its form, probably came from Campache, the Mexican state where a popular furniture mahogany was found.

Thomas Jefferson was sent a campeachy from Louisiana and was most appreciative in his thank-you note, writing, "Age, its infirmities & frequent illnesses have rendered indulgence in that easy kind of chair truly acceptable." Two campeachy chairs at "Monticello," made on the plantation by slave craftsman John Hemings, stood conveniently near the west doors onto the portico and could be carried out easily if needed for comfortable seating.[23]

In common with other skilled carpenters and cabinetmakers on southern plantations, John Hemings enjoyed some degree of autonomy. On one occasion Jefferson wrote asking him to return immediately to "Monticello" from a neighboring plantation where he was working. Writing with the confidence of a master craftsman who would not be hurried (and with the latitude in spelling that was tolerated at the time), Hemings stated firmly, "I hope by the nex to Let you no when I shul finech and when to send for me."[24]

It was not until the 1830s that the rocking chair made its first appearance on porches and in gardens. Purportedly an American invention, the addition of rockers to an ordinary slat back or Windsor chair allowed the American habit of tilting a chair onto its back legs to be done with safety if not elegance.

John Hemings (1775–?). Campeachy chair. Before 1819. Mahogany and leather, 39 x 27 in. Photograph by Edward Owen. Monticello, Thomas Jefferson Memorial Foundation, Charlottesville

The style of building is neat and tidy. Fences and out houses are also in the same style; and being almost universally painted white, make a delightful appearance to the eye.

TIMOTHY DWIGHT, TRAVELS IN NEW-ENGLAND AND NEW-YORK, 1821

ARCADIAN VISIONS, 1810–1840

THE WAR OF 1812 WAS NOT A POPULAR ONE, and its disruption of trade ruined many. It did, however, prove to every citizen's satisfaction the viability of the United States as a nation and reasserted our independence from Britain. At the same time the undermining of the new French Republic by Napoleon's ambition and his adoption of Roman forms tainted them for most Americans. The Greek came to symbolize democracy as the Roman had republicanism, particularly when the modern Greek nation successfully fought the Turks for independence in the early 1820s.

A writer for the *Analectic Magazine* in 1815 patriotically deplored copying English architectural handbooks or even adapting colonial building types, which were considered "always poor and contemptible when compared with the grandeur and the beauty of Grecian simplicity."[1] American architectural pattern books began to feature the Greek orders. John Haviland's *Builder's Assistant* (1818) was the first, but others quickly followed. Architect Asher Benjamin incorporated them into the fifth edition of his ever-popular *The American Builder's Companion* (1826).

Literate Americans, conscious of themselves as citizens of the first modern democracy, understandably felt a kinship with the ancient democracy of Athens. For those classically educated, things Greek represented the highest culture. The imagined Arcadian paradise of ancient Greece, and the simple purity of its architecture was an ideal that was embraced by farmers as well as owners of large estates. The Greek Revival style of architecture was seen as truly modern: it was the first style not derived from English precedent, and it was wholly democratic. Anyone could afford a Greek-style structure—it was

George Flower (1787–1862). GEORGE FLOWER RESIDENCE, ALBION, ILLINOIS. C. 1820.
Watercolor on paper mounted on cardboard, 13 x 17⅜ in. Chicago Historical Society
*The symmetry of George Flower's new house and front garden in the Midwest
with its two circular beds was already going out of fashion in the East.*

easily built in wood, and its trim could be cheaply made from flat, machine-planed boards.

The portico, a symbol of virtue and authority, was affixed to older buildings as well as adorning new ones. Banks and other public buildings seemed replica Parthenons; rectangular colonial homes were entered from the side and given new pediments and pilasters on their gable ends; grand mansions, especially in the South, were built with imposing columned fronts. For the University of Virginia, Thomas Jefferson designed ten different porticos in the Doric, Ionic, or Corinthian orders linked by Tuscan colonnades, all functioning as a three-dimensional textbook of classical styles. By 1834 a correspondent for *The Architectural Magazine* could report that "The Greek mania is at its height, as you infer from the fact that everything is a Greek temple from the privies in the back court through . . . the state house."[2]

GARDEN TEMPLES
Wealthy landowners North and South embraced the Arcadian vision of ancient Greece, and adorned their grounds with imaginative temple replicas. On the grounds of his Greek Revival mansion "Gaineswood" in Demopolis, Alabama, General Nathaniel Whitfield included a circular temple summerhouse. At the entrance to South Carolina Governor John Laurence Manning's Corinthian-columned "Milford" stood a temple gatehouse. The springhouse at "Oaklands," near Baltimore, Maryland, was erected as a two-story temple with four Ionic

columns. At "Bremo" in Fluvanna County, Virginia, John Hartwell Cocke, devastated by the death of his wife in 1816, turned to good works for solace and built a temple springhouse to his wife's memory. More utilitarian springhouses, like that on Schooley's Mountain, a resort in Morris County, New Jersey, also appeared in the guise of temples. Here the "small, neat, wooden structure, with a single apartment and seats for visitors" was adorned with four chaste Doric columns.[3]

The garden privy could be given the dignity of a Grecian facade to match a Greek Revival house. In Natchez, Mississippi, William St. John Elliot built a columned mansion "D'Evereux" in 1836 with a necessary ornamented with corner pilasters supporting an entablature. Like other privies in the South, it had two separate compartments for ladies and gentlemen, entered by doors on opposite sides.[4] Even birdhouses were made in the form of Greek temples—a birdhouse modeled on the Theseum in Athens adorned an outbuilding of a Greek Revival house in Amherst, Massachusetts.[5]

Garden buildings were not always in agreement with the style of the house. General George De Wolfe in 1810 hired Providence architect Russell Warren to design a grand Greek Revival mansion in Bristol, Rhode Island. The summerhouse on the grounds of the general's "The Lindens," however, was the octagonal one with the sprightly bell roof and sculpture finial that had once decorated the garden of his father, Charles, also in Bristol.[6]

When architect Thomas Walter gave Nicholas Biddle's home "Andalusia" an

BELOW, MIDDLE: Privy at "D'Evereux," Natchez, Mississippi. Historic Natchez Foundation
Greek Revival stylistic details, like the corner pilasters supporting an entablature, distinguish the privy built at the suburban Natchez residence of William St. John Elliot in 1836. Separate compartments for men and women were entered on opposite sides.

BELOW, RIGHT: Springhouse and dairy, Goodloe Harper place, Baltimore County. c. 1800. Photograph in *White Pine Series of Architectural Monographs VIII* (1922)
Utilitarian outbuildings, such as this dairy built over a spring, could assume the guise of a garden temple, here with Ionic columns and a decorative entablature and frieze.

William E. Winner
(1815–1883). GARDEN SCENE
NEAR PHILADELPHIA. c. 1840.
Oil on canvas, 16¾ x 21¾ in.
Wadsworth Atheneum,
Hartford, Connecticut. The
Ella Gallup Sumner and
Mary Catlin Sumner
Collection Fund
A cast-iron bench and a column
surmounted with an urn
furnished this flowery corner
of a spacious lawn.

OPPOSITE, TOP: Icehouse,
Githens Farm, Burlington
County, New Jersey. Library
of Congress, Historic
American Buildings Survey,
Washington, D.C.
This appealing icehouse was
given a hexagonal shingled
roof and its obligatory roof vent
made into a decorative steeple.

imposing temple front in 1835, he also designed a mock ruin called the "Grotto" to serve as a ladies' withdrawing room. The gentlemen convened for billiards in a nearby classical temple on this Delaware River estate. John Laurence Manning's imposing Corinthian-columned mansion in South Carolina, begun in 1839, had a temple gatehouse but also a wisteria-draped Gothic folly in the garden.

TRADITIONAL GARDENS NORTH AND SOUTH In the

1810s and 1820s, a taste for Greek Revival architecture, as for gardens in the natural style, was an advanced one. Most gardens in the South followed traditional arrangements, with perhaps a nod to the picturesque. A garden like that of Martha Parke Custis Peter, grand-daughter of Martha Washington and wife of Georgetown tobacco merchant Thomas Peter, was such an example. In 1816, the Peters added a central block with a command-ing classical portico to the existing Federal house on their Georgetown lot, and laid out a garden that combined curving drives and walks in the natural style with a formal knot garden.

Many southern gardens were characterized by a rectangular enclosure for both flowers and vegetables laid out in geometric beds behind or to one side of the house. Sum-

Dovecote, "Bowman's Folly," Accomack County, Virginia. Photograph by Jack E. Boucher, 1960. Library of Congress, Historic American Buildings Survey, Washington, D.C.

merhouses usually marked the crossing of two axial paths in the garden, as did the octagonal one of the 1820s at "Dan's Hill," near Danville, Virginia. Utilitarian outbuildings were grouped conveniently between house and garden, often forming a neat line as at "Bellevue" in Halifax County, Virginia, also dating to the 1820s.[7]

In conservative New England, as in the South, garden layout on small properties usually followed colonial precedent rather than picturesque taste. John Warner Barber in his *Connecticut Historical Collections* (1836) noted of Hartford gardens that "Many of the houses have court yards in front, and gardens in the rear. The former are ornamented with trees and shrubs; the latter are filled with fruit trees, flowers, and culinary vegetables."[8]

Some New Englanders who had established modest fortunes in the economic expansion of the 1820s and 1830s were more up-to-date and built foursquare villas with imposing porticos, as did the Samuel Willistons of Easthampton, Massachusetts. In the 1820s, Emily Williston had begun making covered buttons to help her sheep-farmer husband make ends meet. A lucky sale to a New York merchant led to national orders. Mr. Williston abandoned farming for the more lucrative career of button merchant and in the late 1830s made a fortune by developing the machinery to manufacture the buttons in quantity. He was civic-minded as well as entrepreneurial, and before building his house in Easthampton, Williston endowed a church and school there. The classical portico of his house, begun in 1843, faced the street. To one side was a vine-covered porch looking out to the garden, laid out in geometric beds and backed by a spectacular greenhouse.[9]

More typical was the garden of Charles E. Williams in Deerfield, Massachusetts. Having inherited his father's modest center-hall farmhouse, he contented himself with adding a porch across the front and enclosing his flower garden at the side of his house with a white picket fence entered through an arched trellis. Those who could afford to do so painted their front fences as well as their houses white.

Perhaps Charles Williams's garden contained native flowers as did that of William S. Williams, also in Deerfield. Both Williamses would have had the benefit of the library established in 1821 by the Franklin County Agricultural Society, which included McMahon's *American Gardener's Calendar* (1806), and Thomas Fessenden's *The New*

England Farmer (1824) and his *The New American Gardener* (1828).[10] The latter book contained nurseryman André Parmentier's short essay "Landscapes and Picturesque Gardens," advocating the natural style in gardening.

FRONTIER GARDENS Settlers in the Western Reserve and farther West along the Great Lakes tended to follow conservative New England precedents in both house and garden. Margaret Fuller, a member of the Transcendental circle around Ralph Waldo Emerson and a writer for *The Dial,* spent the summer of 1843 making a tour of the Great Lakes from Niagara Falls, New York, to Wisconsin and Illinois. Her description of Niagara was tempered by the picturesque aesthetic and the many paintings of the Falls she had seen; she wrote, "I knew where to look for everything, and everything looked as I thought it would."

As she traveled farther west, the land assumed in her eyes the aspect of "a garden interspersed with cottages, groves and flowery lawns." It was the great openness and expanse of the landscape, so unlike that of New England, that excited her greatest admiration. She exclaimed, "Here a man need not take a small slice from the landscape, and fence it in . . . and there cut down his fancies to miniature improvements which a chicken could run over in ten minutes . . . . He can afford to leave some of it wild, and carry out his own plans without obliterating those of nature." Nonetheless, she noted that settlers had brought with them flowers and occasionally trees from the East, and that even the smallest log cabins often had a traditional flower garden in front.[11]

The first settlers from New England were established in Marietta, Ohio, in 1788. As a later history pointed out, the houses there were "constructed with great neatness, having fine gardens, and ornamental trees and shrubbery, which mark the New England origins of its population."[12] Even so, the Arcadian vision accompanied many of the settlers, and was expressed in their choice of style for their house, if not in their gardens. The Mills garden in Marietta, for example, was laid out in 1814 in descending terraces from the Greek Revival house sited on a hill. A latticed summerhouse next to the house overlooked the flower parterre arranged in geometric beds.[13]

The earliest settlers in the prairie states were often people of some means as it took a substantial investment in oxen, Cyrus McCormick's newly invented steel-bottom plow, and several years of cultivation before the grassland became profitable. Variations on Classical Revival structures known back East were built there and in established settlements along the expanding frontier well into the 1860s.[14]

Most home grounds on the frontier were strictly functional, with outbuildings

Robert Hanna (1789–1854). WHEELING AND WHEELING ISLAND. c. 1838. Oil on canvas, 23¾ x 32½ in. Oglebay Institute, Mansion Museum, Wheeling, West Virginia *Hanna bought the brick house in Bridgeport, Ohio, seen on the right in 1829. The fretwork gate leading to the house is painted white as is the wooden addition.*

near the house limited to a wooden smokehouse and privy. Pigeon raising was common in the southern territories, and a small octagonal pigeon house elevated on a pole would have provided a decorative accent. The kitchen garden might have had a grape arbor and included flowers, particularly sunflowers and hollyhocks, along one side.[15]

As territories became more settled, local residents increasingly had the income to build houses in the modern Greek style and to make gardens incorporating picturesque structures and natural plantings. The Territory of Arkansas, established in 1819, had both nurserymen and pleasure gardens by the 1830s. William E. Woodruff, editor of the *Arkansas Gazette,* began Little Rock's first seed company in 1828. His new brick house, built directly on the street, had both a flower and vegetable garden on its east side. Woodruff's daughter described the gardens as they were in her childhood: "A little portico covered in vines and roses opened on a walk which led to the summer house, and near it stood a pear tree over which a coral honeysuckle and a climbing rose contended for possession. . . . A trumpet creeper covered the carriage house climbing over to the pigeon house above, making the otherwise homely building beautiful to behold. . . . A grape arbor ran across the garden and through it passed a trough conducting water to the lot."[16]

Albert Pike, a poet in Little Rock, Arkansas, in an article for the *American Monthly Magazine* in 1836 wrote disdainfully of the old style of gardening with beds "laid out, formally, in squares and parallelograms . . . wherein art hath not so far advanced as to seem like nature." His Greek Revival home, built in 1840, predictably had grounds in the natural style where, as described by a visitor in 1857, "shrubbery and exotics of choice varieties are scattered with a profuse hand."[17]

THE PICTURESQUE ITINERARY America's uniqueness as a modern-day democracy was felt to be rooted in the special nature of the North American continent. Assertive nationalism and democratic ideals combined in embracing both Arcadian Greece and the native landscape of America. As an essayist in *The Port Folio,* an influential Philadelphia periodical, predicted in 1812: "our artists, instead of servilely imitating the works of European masters, will boldly pursue the same course as the ancient Grecians, who had nature only for their model, and genius for their guide."[18] Painters, led by Thomas Cole, sought to free themselves from European conventions and devise a distinctively American view of the native landscape.

Daniel Wadsworth of Hartford, an early patron of Cole, commissioned from the painter in 1828 a distant prospect of his country estate "Montevideo" and its battlemented Gothic cottage. The picturesque grounds held a fifty-five-foot-high hexagonal wooden tower with a crenelated observation platform from which to view the nearby ornamental plantings and small lake, as well as the distant vista of the Connecticut River Valley.[19] From the Gothic windows of the house itself, visitors could enjoy prospects of both mountain solitude and the settled river valley, the sublime and the picturesque in a distinctly American combination.

The spread of railroads along the coast, the establishment of steamboat lines up the Hudson River, and the opening of the Erie Canal in 1825 meant that Americans interested in viewing natural scenery at first hand could do so with relative ease. Portfolios of engravings depicting picturesque locales begin to appear in the 1820s, most notably Joshua Shaw's *Picturesque Views of American Scenery* and William Guy Wall's *Hudson River Portfolio.* Even earlier, writers had described picturesque itineraries in scenic locales, as did theologian Timothy Dwight of the environs of Lake George in 1802. Here, from the "best points of view," he admired the "solemn and forbidding" mountains and the "unceasing variegations of light and shade" of their cloaking forests, as well as the settlements that transformed the sublime landscape into a picturesque one.[20]

Such journeys in search of the picturesque had been popularized in England through the writings of the Rev. William Gilpin, who described views with contrasting elements, composed in an orderly transition from detailed foreground to generalized distance, that would look well in a landscape painting. He prized ruins as focal points, writing that "Among all the objects of art, the picturesque eye is perhaps most inquisitive after the elegant relics of ancient architecture; the ruined tower, the Gothic arch, the remains of castles and abbeys."[21] Gothic architecture was viewed by all as intrinsically picturesque, as its fragmented, irregular forms, activated surfaces, and interlaced shapes recalled natural growth.

RUINS AND THE PICTURESQUE LANDSCAPE
The simple geometric forms and clear outlines of Classical Revival structures could increasingly be found in grounds laid out in a picturesque manner as a romantic sensibility began to undermine rational neoclassicism. Popular novels romanticized both the classical and the medieval past; Edward Bulwer Lytton's riveting *The Last Days of Pompeii* (1834) was equalled in popularity by Sir Walter Scott's Waverley novels.

The presence of sham ruins indicated unmistakably a desire to create a romantic, picturesque setting for the home. A townscape of Stonington, Connecticut, painted in the early 1800s, shows a decayed battlement as the gateway to a Greek Revival mansion approached by a curving path. In an extreme example, John Church Cruger imported a Mayan ruin from Mexico to ornament his grounds on an island in the Hudson north of Tarrytown, New York. Ruins even appeared within the house—paintings and prints of romantic landscapes with crenelated towers or Gothic ruins not only decorated the walls but ornamented the backs of many American Empire chairs.

Fort Ticonderoga, a ready-made ruin redolent with associations, overlooked William Pell's Classical Revival home built in 1826 on the shores of Lake Champlain. Timothy Dwight's son Theodore included Fort Ticonderoga on his northern tour in search of the picturesque, and recorded that Pell had planted thousands of black locust and chestnut trees as well as catalpas, tulip poplars, and hundreds of fruit trees in the formerly open fields around his villa.[22] These groves of trees would furnish the variety of shapes and ever-shifting patterns of light and shade so desirable in the picturesque landscape.

Sir Walter Scott's home, "Abbotsford," dramatically sited on the banks of the River Tweed in Scotland with a picturesque garden created in the 1810s, had a demonstrable influence on such gardens in America. In his 1813 poem "The Bride of Triermain," Scott described a medieval garden "Flank'd by some castle's Gothic round":

> Fain would the artist's skill provide,
> The limits of his realms to hide.
> The walks in labyrinths he twines,
> Shade after shade with skill combines,
> With many a varied flowing knot,
> And copse, and arbor decks the spot . . .

Thomas Cole (1801–1848). VIEW OF MONTEVIDEO. 1828. Oil on panel, 19¾ x 26¹/₁₆ in. Wadsworth Atheneum, Hartford, Connecticut. Bequest of Daniel Wadsworth *Daniel Wadsworth began his Gothic Revival house "Montevideo" at Avon, Connecticut, in 1805. Cole contrasted the wilderness, with its blasted tree on the left seen in shadow, with the sunlit house and distant settled valley on the right.*

George Inness (1825–1894).
SUNNYSIDE. c. 1850–60. Oil on
canvas, 14¾ x 19¾ in. Historic
Hudson Valley, Tarrytown,
New York
*Inness emphasized the
picturesque surroundings of
"Sunnyside," such as the
luxuriant vines clothing the
house and the venerable trees
that provided moving contrasts
of light and shadow.*

Robert Gilmore visited "Abbotsford," as well as Horace Walpole's Gothic fantasy "Strawberry Hill" at Twickenham. An admirer of the picturesque, in 1832 he had architect Alexander Jackson Davis design for property near Baltimore an asymmetrical Gothic house, "Glen Ellen," set in a lawn with trees clustered in a picturesque manner. Significantly its gatehouse masqueraded as a Gothic ruin. James Fenimore Cooper returned from a visit to "Abbotsford" in 1833 and gave his "Otsego Hall" at Cooperstown, New York, a Gothic porch and crenelated parapet.

"SUNNYSIDE"   Washington Irving also visited "Abbotsford," and in 1835 began remodeling his recently purchased old Dutch cottage, "Sunny-

side," at Tarrytown on the Hudson. He was aided by his friend, landscape painter George Harvey, who had the previous year built a Gothic house in nearby Hastings-on-Hudson with a garden laid out in the picturesque manner.

For Irving, "Sunnyside" was as much an imaginative historical construction as were his legends of New York history. His renovations to the house mark the beginning of the change in American domestic architecture from the Greek Revival to a picturesque style characterized by irregularity, variety, and promiscuous borrowings from the past. Just as Sir Walter Scott had expanded "Abbotsford" into a medieval fantasy, Irving transformed his unprepossessing stone cottage into a commodious manor evoking the romance

Anonymous. TOWNSCAPE, STONINGTON, CONNECTICUT. c. 1800–25. Watercolor on paper, 18 x 22 in. Shelburne Museum, Vermont (27.2.2–8)

Thomas Chipman. CARILLON
AND THE RUINS OF TICONDERO-
GA. 1827. Engraving, 4⅞ x 8¼
in. Fort Ticonderoga Museum,
New York
*Steamboats on Lake Champlain
made it comparatively easy to
visit such scenic locations as
Fort Ticonderoga.*

BELOW: Gothic bench. 1836.
Cast iron, 49½ x 30½ x 19 in.
Historic Hudson Valley,
Tarrytown, New York
*Designed by Washington Irving,
this bench was cast as one of a
pair by the West Point Foundry,
Cold Spring, as a gift for
"Sunnyside."*

of early Dutch settlement in the Hudson River Valley.

The varied forms and picturesque outlines of Irving's cottage found an echo in the verdant surroundings he devised for it in a conscious affiliation of his home grounds with the American past and the American landscape.[23] He began by planting both ornamental and fruit trees and by 1838 had established a kitchen garden and flower beds. He reported laying out lawns, "sunny walks . . . secluded walks, quiet glens and sheltering groves."[24] One of the walks led to a massive tree called the "Haunted Oak" beside a stream in a wooded ravine; other paths went along the riverfront and provided distant vistas.

The honeysuckle, roses, and ivy (reputedly from a cutting taken at "Abbotsford") had taken hold, and Irving wrote that they were "clothing the cottage with verdure" in an appropriately picturesque manner.[25] Artist T. Addison Richards, who visited and made sketches in 1856, marveled that although the acres were few "yet so varied is their surface, so richly wooded and flowered, and so full of elfish winding paths and grassy lanes, exploring hillsides and chasing merry brooks that their numbers seem to be countless."[26] Rustic seats were placed at convenient points along the garden paths, but Irving's porch had more formal seating, two cast-iron benches in the Gothic style. The benches, a gift of the owner of the West Point Foundry, were made after a design supplied by Irving himself.[27]

In the country there is no necessity for large parlors—the garden is the country parlor. Our drawing-rooms are deserted by our friends and visitors—they are to be found examining our rare shrubs and flowers—promenading our garden walks—reclining on the lawn, enjoying the grateful shade and cooling breeze. How necessary, then that our garden furniture should be convenient and appropriate; that proper resting places be provided, to insure the fullest enjoyment of the garden by ourselves and our friends.

"Garden Furniture," The Horticulturist, July 1853

PICTURESQUE GARDENS
and RUSTIC SEATS, 1840–1870

B Y 1840, RAPID INDUSTRIALIZATION AND THE growth of cities had made the Arcadian vision seem a vanished ideal as the tide of Jacksonian populism overwhelmed ancient values and virtues. Even in the new western territories, land speculation and entrepreneurial enterprise kept pace with agriculture. Classically derived architecture remained popular, especially in the South and in new towns on the western frontier, although for many it no longer seemed to reflect the expansive optimism that accompanied economic recovery from the Panic of 1837.

The gradual fall from favor of Greek Revival architecture and the eventual triumph of the picturesque in both house and garden were largely due to the combined talents and vision of architect Alexander Jackson Davis and nurseryman Andrew Jackson Downing. Downing was able to congratulate himself in his new magazine *The Horticulturist* in 1846 that "the Greek Temple disease has passed its crisis. The people have survived it," but warned of a second disease, "the mania just springing up for a kind of *spurious* rural gothic cottage."[1]

Davis, who had studied landscape painting, gained his knowledge of architecture and landscape gardening through his association with architect Ithiel Town and his reading in Town's extensive library. As was the case with so many educated and influential Americans before the Civil War, Davis never visited Europe. His house pattern book *Rural Residences* (1837) was among the first in a long line of design books aimed at homeowners rather than builders. Like the shelter magazines of today, these pattern books allowed homeowners to plan structures in the latest style. The new technology of

Frederick Elmore Cohen (c. 1818–1858). BENTLEY SIMONS RUNYAN FAMILY. c. 1857–58. Oil on canvas, 38 x 45 in. Allen Memorial Art Museum, Oberlin College, Ohio. Gift of Mrs. James C. McCullough, 1970
The Runyans of Mansfield, Ohio, filled their front and side yards with hopeful little trees and shrubs that, together with the vines trained on the trellises, would soften the austere lines of the Greek Revival house, painted an atypical pale green.

balloon frame construction, which made it easy to build asymmetrical designs, gave a boost to picturesque structures.

Davis's designs for Gothic cottages and villas all appeared in landscape settings—an important feature of most designs was a veranda from which to view the grounds. This integration of picturesque buildings and their landscape setting was a principle advocated by Davis's friend and collaborator, Andrew Jackson Downing.

Downing, whose nursery was in Newburgh, New York, had learned the natural style of landscape gardening through the publications of English designers Humphrey Repton and John Claudius Loudon, and through visits to estates along the Hudson River and elsewhere. He did not get to England until 1850.

The year after the publication of Davis's designs, Downing wrote asking him for help with a projected book of his own. Six of Davis's designs were subsequently published in Downing's immensely influential *Treatise on the Theory and Practice of Landscape Gardening Adapted to North America* (1841). Downing's ability to articulate complex aesthetic principles clearly and forcefully, paired with Davis's convincing illustrations of their application, firmly established the ideal of the picturesque rural residence in the minds of the thousands of Americans who read the *Treatise* in its many editions, and followed articles in Downing's magazine *The Horticulturist*.

THE PICTURESQUE GARDEN
For Downing, laying out grounds in a picturesque fashion was a democratic art rooted in the American soil and equivalent to the search of painters and writers for both national and personal meaning in the natural landscape. Just as the picturesque natural landscape seen on the painter's canvas was characterized by strong contrasts of light and shade, animated surfaces, and complex and varied masses in an asymmetrical arrangement so was the picturesque garden. Like landscape paintings, picturesque gardens were laid out in a sequential narrative, microcosms of managed nature to be experienced in the course of picturesque itineraries in miniature. As a critic for the *Bulletin of the American Art Union* wrote in 1849, "in all landscapes there must be a direct road where the eye shall naturally fall . . . this must be a grand plot, to which all incidents, hills, trees, etc. must relate."[2]

Robert Donaldson's "Blithewood" on the Hudson, and the adjoining estate "Montgomery Place," where Davis added pavilions and garden structures through the 1840s, and to which Downing may have given advice as well as supplying plants, exemplified the picturesque landscape for both Davis and Downing. Downing's account of "A Visit to Montgomery Place" published in *The Horticulturist* (1847) enables us to follow a planned picturesque itinerary through the grounds.

Beginning from the manicured lawn with its river view, the itinerary of the Morning Walk led to a "fanciful rustic-gabled seat" in a locust grove and then downward to a "Deeply shaded, winding" path along the bank interrupted by unexpected vistas. Rustic seats occurred at particularly picturesque locales. A longer itinerary led through The Wilderness, a wooded valley "much varied in surface" with a "mountain torrent" at the bottom. Ascending a stair in the "precipitous banks" led to an "airy looking rustic bridge" spanning the stream. Upstream was The Lake, "half overhung and deeply shaded by the bowery thickets" and ornamented by a rustic temple, best seen "either toward evening, or in moonlight . . . [when] the effect of contrast in light and shadow is most striking. . . ."[3] Time of day was an important consideration for picturesque viewing. In an account of a visit to Nathaniel Parker Willis's "Idlewild," the author regretted that he had arrived at noon "when nature is *en dishabille* and all her shadows off."[4]

"Blithewood" and "Montgomery Place" were both estates of many acres. It was, however, Downing's contention—often expressed in the pages of his magazine *The Horticulturist,* and in two house pattern books, *Cottage Residences* (1842) and *The Architecture of Country Houses* (1850)—that picturesque grounds could also be made on a small scale. He felt small properties ought to be limited to lawn and judiciously placed groups of trees and shrubs. The walks through the grounds ought to be curved so that "a new turn in the

George Harvey (1803–1892). GATE-HOUSE IN THE RUSTIC COTTAGE STYLE. 1836. Lithograph, 13½ x 9⅝ in. Avery Architectural and Fine Arts Library, Columbia University, New York *Alexander Jackson Davis designed this board-and-batten Gothic cottage for the entrance to "Blithewood." Finials and scalloped bargeboards ornamented the steep gables.*

walk opens a new prospect . . . continually offering new freshment and variety."[5]

Downing preferred rustic garden ornaments to those mass produced, remarking, "They have the merit of being tasteful and picturesque in their appearance and are easily constructed by the amateur." He recommended arbors to give an "impression of refinement and taste" and the generous use of vines, which signaled "domesticity and the presence of heart."[6] Such rustic garden structures had the natural tones preferred by a picturesque taste that abhorred the color white for buildings, fences, or anything at all. As James Fenimore Cooper wrote in the *Home Book of the Picturesque,* "A fence that looks as if it were covered with clothes hung up to dry, does very little towards aiding the picturesque."[7]

Downing's own "Highland Gardens" in Newburgh, its Tudor-style house and surrounding garden occupying less than half of the four-acre property, was described in *The Horticulturist* following Downing's untimely death in 1852. Just within the Gothic entrance gate was a rustic trellis which framed "a lovely picture of the river and the Fishkill mountains. . . ." The house was approached by a curving carriage road from which a footpath branched, running the length of the garden. It was flanked on one side with shrubbery arranged to allow river views, and on the other by the tree-shaded lawn. Also visible from the path was a sundial which, as such objects were intended to do, elicited

Alexander Jackson Davis
(1803–1880). RAVINE WALK,
BLITHEWOOD. n.d. Ink and
wash on paper, 6¾ x 4½ in.
Avery Architectural and
Fine Arts Library, Columbia
University, New York
*Gloomy ravines spanned by
rustic bridges were a staple of
the picturesque garden. Davis
may have designed this one with
its rustic gazebo for Robert
Donaldson's "Blithewood,"
Annandale-on-Hudson.*

in the visitor a chain of melancholy associations. A dense shrubbery threaded by a serpentine path terminated in a rustic hermitage. Continuing on the main path the visitor
encountered another lawn studded with flower beds and backed with flowering shrubs.
From the seat in a rustic arbor by the side of the path the visitor could enjoy the distant
mountains and the pastoral riverside settlements.[8]

"THE HIGHLANDS" Among the historic gardens added
to the 1844 second edition of Downing's *Treatise* was that of "The Highlands" in
Whitemarsh (Fort Washington), Pennsylvania, bought by George Sheaff in 1808. A
vignette showed the front of the house and the "magnificent white oak" which Downing felt gave "an air of dignity to the whole place."[9] Visible in the wood engraving is a

rustic bench around the tree trunk, an arbor covered with vines, and a flower bed in the shape of a basket. No mention was made of the most conspicuous feature of the garden, a crenelated stone wall flanked by two Gothic pavilions. These may have been built in the 1840s when Sheaff offered the property for sale and mentioned a "grape wall."[10]

The garden was a consuming interest not just for George Sheaff but also for his wife, Katherine, who wrote of the garden in her diaries of the 1830s and 1840s. On April 20, 1838, she lamented a late freeze with the exclamation, "Florida! Florida! wherefore art thou, not Whitemarsh!" and recorded with joy the first wild flowers. July 4th that year was celebrated with "an animated dance in the verandah" that spilled over into the garden. On January 20, 1842, she noted that fifty peach trees from McMahon's nursery had been planted in rows along the carriage road.[11] Often recorded was the seemingly never-ending task of making jams and jellies from these peaches and other soft fruits planted in the garden.

ABOVE: Osgood-Brockway garden, Newburyport, Massachusetts. Photograph by H. P. Macintosh, c. 1859. Society for the Preservation of New England Antiquities, Boston
In 1842, John Osgood and Charles Brockway bought the house and probably laid out the flower garden of box-bordered geometric beds. The central path led through the flower parterre and under a latticed wisteria arbor to three terraces planted with flowers and fruit trees.

"The Highlands" wall and garden house. Photograph, c. 1920. The Highlands, Fort Washington, Pennsylvania
The crenelated wall, intended for grapes, and its Gothic garden house date to the 1840s. The photograph documents the garden's appearance after 1917, when the Sheaff estate was bought by Miss Caroline Sinkler.

Wheelwright garden, Newburyport, Massachusetts. Photograph by Philip Coombs, early 1860s. Society for the Preservation of New England Antiquities, Boston
The Gothic summerhouse, probably built in 1841, seems to have provoked a rash of such structures in Newburyport gardens. A latticed fence screened the barnyard on the right.

NEW ENGLAND PICTURESQUE Downing's influence was far-reaching. Author Catharine Sedgwick commented that "nobody whether he be rich or poor, builds a house or lays out a garden without consulting Downing's works."[12] Even so, an article in *The Horticulturist* pointed out that New England at least seemed immune to his influence: "the taste of New England people generally, for the beautiful and picturesque in landscape scenery is either vitiated, or totally uncultivated. Hence the great mass of the people prefer symmetry, stiff formality, straight lines, and the geometrical forms of the ancient or artificial style of laying out grounds."[13]

Many small gardens laid out in New England in the 1840s do have geometrical or arabesque flower beds as principle features but also the serpentine paths, ornamental clumps of trees and shrubs, and variety of levels characteristic of the picturesque landscape. Gardens in Newburyport, Massachusetts, for example, boast a fascinating range of Gothic latticed garden houses as well as multilevel arrangements and intricate patterned beds.

The William Wheelwright garden on Newburyport High Street is documented in a photograph of the 1860s. Here a Gothic summerhouse, crowned by a scale model of the Old South Church in Newburyport, straddled a path lined with roses, marking a change of level from the patterned box-edged perennial beds to a lower orchard and vegetable garden. According to the Historic American Buildings Survey, the garden was laid out when William Wheelwright bought the house in 1841. Wheelwright, although for the most part absent in South America and London on business, maintained strong friendships with Newburyport residents, particularly Caleb Cushing, whose garden was nearby.[14]

Cushing had read "with great delight" Washington Irving's *Sketchbook of Geoffrey Crayon,* which set him on his own European tour in search of the picturesque; he met Irving himself in Paris in 1829. The following year Cushing returned from France with a design for his own arabesque garden parterre, which he surrounded with a picturesque arrangement of native trees and shrubs gathered from all over New England. One native, the Oregon grape holly, was reputedly started from a cutting taken from Sir Walter Scott's "Abbotsford."[15]

The garden of the neighboring William Moulton house, like that of the Wheelwright house, occupied a long, relatively narrow lot. The flower garden, probably dating to the 1840s, was to the left of a path from the house that passed through a grape arbor to the orchard in back. The latticed garden house was sited in the far corner of the flower garden outside the box-edged beds; the privy, screened with lattice, occupied the corner near the house. A simpler latticed house was placed as the terminus of a path through the orchard to the back fence. A pointed arch marked the entrance to the flower garden, and another led from the far end of the box-edged perennial beds.[16]

OLD-FASHIONED GARDENS
More conservative gardeners both in New England and the South retained traditional garden plans. Alexander Hamilton Ladd inherited an eighteenth-century house and garden in Portsmouth,

Marie Adrien Persac (1822/24–1873). THE OLIVIER PLANTATION, LOUISIANA. 1861. Watercolor, 16 x 22 in. On loan to the Louisiana State Museum, New Orleans
Many of the outbuildings necessary on a self-sufficient sugar plantation can be seen in this delightful view. Two cisterns to catch rainwater from the roof stand within the picket fence circling the house. Next to the overseer's cabin, a bell tower and dovecote are balanced by the stables, smokehouse, and other offices on the left.

William Moulton Garden, Newburyport, Massachusetts. Photograph by Mary H. Northend, c. 1890. Society for the Preservation of New England Antiquities, Boston *The geometric flower beds here were simpler than those of the Wheelwright garden, but were also bordered in dwarf box. Lattice was used in the construction of summerhouses and arbors as well as to screen the privy. The Gothic arch is covered in Virginia creeper.*

New Hampshire, in 1862. The garden, rising in four terraces to the back gate, was bisected by a wide path. To this formal structure Ladd added a winding path along the north boundary wall and planted shrubs and fruit trees, along with wisteria to clothe the west side of the house. He also built arbors for grapes and a distinctive spiral trellis for climbing roses, and contrived a wooden structure to house his beehives.[17]

The grounds of "Westend" in Louisa County, Virginia, planned by Mrs. James Watson in the late 1840s, had a Downing-influenced lawn with groupings of trees, but there was an avenue of elms leading to the house, and the combined flower and vegetable garden took the traditional rectangular form. The summerhouse was placed on the axial path at the division between flower and vegetable beds. John Coles Rutherford, who had visited Europe and had a keen interest in landscape gardening, planted trees and shrubs in the picturesque manner at "Rock Castle" in Goochland County, Virginia. His flower and vegetable garden, however, was planted in squares and enclosed in a white picket fence entered through a rose arbor.[18]

Tennessee, on the frontier at the end of the eighteenth century, by the 1840s had notable gardens. President Andrew Jackson in 1836 commissioned Robert Mills to add a Corinthian portico to "The Hermitage" near Nashville. Both flowers and vegetables were included in the garden laid out in four symmetrical beds. Nearby "Cleveland Hall," built

T. K. Wharton. "The Elms,"
Natchez, Mississippi. 1859.
Pencil on paper, 8 x 10 in. Collection Mrs. Alma Carpenter
*"The Elms," built in 1804, was
enlarged several times and in
the 1850s given a Greek Revival
billiard hall. The hexagonal
latticed summerhouse to the right
of the house may be of the same
date. To the left, the remains of a
conservatory form a picturesque
ivy-covered ruin.*

in 1841, had an equally traditional garden, symmetrical in arrangement with an open summerhouse covered in jasmine terminating the main axis.[19]

MOVING WEST   William B. Wait, Arkansas's first profession-
al banker, in the 1850s laid out a garden to one side of his house in Little Rock that combined an informal planting of trees and shrubs, flowers, and a rustic arbor with an extensive
vegetable garden arranged in rectangular beds bordered by a hedge. Behind the garden,
the barnyard was screened by a long grape arbor with privies at each end. In the rear of
the house, conveniently arranged outbuildings included a smokehouse and well house.[20]

Robert Campbell journeyed from Ireland to St. Louis, Missouri, in 1824 seeking
his fortune. He left St. Louis for the Great Plains where he joined in the lucrative fur
trade and established the Rocky Mountain Fur Company with partners including the
legendary guide Kit Carson. (Campbell became something of a legend himself; Washington
Irving wrote that his "adventures and exploits partake of the wildest spirit of romance."[21])
Returning to St. Louis a wealthy man, he married and in 1854 bought a house in suburban Lucas Place. Here on an adjacent lot he built a classically inspired lattice summerhouse and trellis wall separating a formal front garden from the stable yard.

RIGHT: William B. Wait house and garden, Little Rock. Photograph, 1860s. Arkansas History Commission, Little Rock
William Wait's house can be seen behind the trees and shrubs that filled his garden. The picket fence in the foreground is one of many imaginative variations used at this time.

BELOW, LEFT: Campbell House, summerhouse and trellis. Photograph, c. 1930. Campbell House Foundation, St. Louis
Although the proportions and arched openings of Robert Campbell's summerhouse and arbor are classical, the gable is ornamented with a scalloped bargeboard, and airy jigsaw panels form pillars and frieze.

RIGHT: "Residence of Thomas Gaff, Aurora, Indiana." Engraving in *Atlas of Dearborn County* (1875). Hillforest Historical Foundation, Indiana
The grounds of "Hillforest" occupied a ten-acre hillside threaded with curving drives through groves of trees. Barely visible in the upper right is a rustic bridge that crossed a ravine and led to a rustic summerhouse.

By contrast, the garden of "Hillforest" in Aurora, Indiana, laid out in 1852, exemplified the picturesque style. Thomas Gaff, a shipper and steamboat owner, surrounded his delightful Tuscan villa with curving paths, Downingesque plantings, and rustic outbuildings, including a summerhouse and a "melon house," a stone structure with a rustic table and benches on its flat roof.

Minnesota had been designated a territory in 1849, setting off a wave of immigration and the founding of hundreds of new towns. William LeDuc came to St. Paul in 1850 and by 1864 was affluent enough to build a house in suburban Hastings based on the "Cottage in the Rhine Style" in Downing's *Cottage Residences*. His landscaping was equally picturesque with a curving drive, mature oaks and conifers, and a vine-screened porch.[22]

FARM AND COTTAGE Downing's opinions to the contrary, many felt his designs were inappropriate for small properties. A reader of *The Cultivator* in 1847 complained that "There is something needed to meet the wants of the mechanic and farming community. Mr. Downing's designs and plans are too expensive for general use among this class of persons; they will do for what are termed gentlemen farmers . . . but we want something for the industrious working man." Nonetheless, even *The Cultivator* published Downingesque plans for garden layouts, in part due to the magazine's publisher, Luther Tucker. In 1846 Tucker began a new journal, *The Horticulturist,* with Downing as editor. In his editorials, more than in the *Treatise,* Downing advocated moderation and simplicity, with house and grounds appropriate to an individual's occupation and style of life.[23]

In the wake of Downing's publications, architectural pattern books such as *The Working-Man's Cottage Architecture* (1848), magazines, and gardening manuals aimed at farmers and laborers were published. Walter Elder, former gardener for Robert Donaldson at "Blithewood," listed at the beginning of his *The Cottage Garden of America* (1856) American writers on horticulture, among them Downing. All of them, he pointed out, "address the inhabitants of the *mansion*." Elder considered himself the first writer on gardens to "address ourselves entirely to the intelligent *cottagers* of America."[24]

Solon Robinson, who had been a pioneer farmer in Indiana in the 1830s, wrote for farm magazines in the 1840s before becoming agriculture editor for the *New York Tribune* in 1853. He was the author of the admonitory text *How to Live: Saving and Wasting, or Domestic Economy* (1860) that contrasted a spendthrift and unhappy city family with a rural one living sensibly and comfortably. In 1846 he published an article, "A Cheap Farm House," in *The Cultivator* in which he commented that Downing's ideas were suited only to the "upper ten thousand" of those who lived in the countryside, and proposed for real farmers piecemeal construction of farmhouses and outbuildings using the inexpensive balloon frame.[25]

Lewis F. Allen's *Rural Architecture* (1853) likewise aimed to give sensible plans for homes and outbuildings prizing efficiency over beauty. Among the outbuildings that Allen championed was the privy. As he exhorted, "watercloets have no business in a farmer's house. They are an *effeminancy* only, and introduced by city life."[26] Later pattern books continued to suggest designs for privies, some in the Gothic style. *Woodward's Architecture and Rural Art* (1867), for example, included among Gothic outbuildings a toolshed/privy combination as well as rustic icehouses and oriental summerhouses.

On farms where there were keen flower gardeners, privies were often treated as an important garden feature. Writing of her childhood on a homestead in northern Minnesota, Emily Polasek recalled that "Mother planted hollyhocks, larkspur and Oriental poppies around the house, had a big flower garden by the barn, and even planted flowers around the outhouse."[27]

GOTHIC CASTLES AND COTTAGES Although Downing had advocated the Gothic style for its moral associations as well as for its picturesque qualities, it remained a specialized taste. An 1847 review of William H. Ranlett's Gothic house designs (published 1849–51 as *The American Architect*) protested that "It was quite pardonable in Horace Walpole and Sir Walter Scott to build gingerbread houses in imitation of robber barons and Bluebeard chieftains; they were poets and had written Gothic romances. . . . But there can be nothing more grotesque, more absurd or more affected than for a quiet gentleman, who has made his fortune in the peaceful occupation of selling calicos, and who knows no more of the middle ages than they do of him, to erect for his family a gimcrack of a Gothic castle."[28] Nonetheless a surprising number of merchants built themselves Gothic cottages, if not castles, with picturesque gardens to match. Perhaps they sought the cachet associated with a style that, in the 1840s and 1850s, marked them as men of virtue, cultivation, and advanced taste, as the Greek style had done in the 1820s and 1830s.

In 1854 Joseph Warren Revere returned from adventuring in California and Mexico to build a house in Morris Township, New Jersey, copied from a Gothic design

in Gervase Wheeler's *Rural Homes* (1851). Cornelius Tyler Longstreet, a wealthy businessman, commissioned James Renwick, Jr., architect of the Smithsonian Castle in Washington, D.C., to design for a hilltop in Syracuse, New York, a Gothic mansion completed in 1854. The grounds, ornamented with appropriate structures including a Gothic summerhouse, were laid out in the picturesque style.[29]

Justin Smith Morrill, the son of a blacksmith in Strafford, Vermont, left school at fifteen to clerk in a store and was soon taken into partnership. The business prospered under his care and in 1848 he was able to sell his interest and retire to plan and build his Gothic house and garden in Strafford, completed in time for his marriage in 1851 at age forty-one. Following Downing's principles, Morrill aimed for unity of house and grounds. The cottage was surrounded with a lawn and specimen trees, with vegetable garden, woodlot, orchard, and pond—all part of a carefully considered whole. Flowers were confined to round- and star-shaped beds along the walks.[30]

Henry Chandler Bowen, a prominent silk merchant in Brooklyn, New York, commissioned architect Joseph Wells in 1845 to build a Gothic cottage for him facing the town common in his hometown of Woodstock, Connecticut. Downing had advised those with small places to conceal the boundary lines with trees and shrubs in irregular group-

Anonymous. ROSELAND COTTAGE, HENRY BOWEN HOUSE, WOODSTOCK, CONNECTICUT. c. 1850. Watercolor on paper, 12¾ x 17¾ in. Society for the Preservation of New England Antiquities, Boston. Henry Bowen House, Woodstock, Connecticut. Gift of Margaret Carson Holt (1970.442)
The picket fence along the road and the latticed arbor at the entrance to the enclosed flower garden were already in place in this view of Henry Chandler Bowen's "Roseland Cottage," begun in 1845.

Joseph Lee (1827–1880).
RALSTON HALL AND ITS
GROUNDS, SAN MATEO COUNTY,
CALIFORNIA. c. 1858–65. Oil on
canvas, 30 x 47⅞ in. Hirschl
& Adler Galleries, Inc., New
York
*In 1864 Count Leonetto Cipriani
sold his estate overlooking the
San Francisco bay to W. C.
Ralston. It included an enclosed
garden around the stone house as
well as numerous outbuildings,
among them an observation
tower.*

ings. Among Bowen's first recorded purchases in 1847 were fruit trees and the spiry-topped conifers like fir and larch considered by Downing to be particularly suited to the Gothic style.

In 1850 Bowen bought pickets for a fence along the road, and 128 bush honeysuckles to cover them. He also bought six hundred yards of dwarf boxwood to surround the beds of the flower parterre to the south of the house.[31] One entered the flower garden through a latticed arbor, which was enclosed with a lattice fence. The garden house to one side of the flower parterre was a simplified temple enclosed in lattice.

The longing for perfect, geometric forms, left unsatisfied by the picturesque, found outlets in the garden where classical temples or other geometric structures were still being built as summerhouses. A few house pattern books continued to advocate such geometric buildings. Most notably Orson Squire Fowler's *A Home for All* (1848 and subsequent editions) proposed the octagon for houses, arguing that the Gothic was undemocratic and eccentric and appropriate only for wealthy aesthetes. Fowler (also a phrenologist and the author of two bestselling sex manuals) considered the octagon to be the most beautiful form for building as it most nearly approached the circle.[32]

GOTHIC PAVILIONS   In the conservative South, Gothic garden structures occasionally accompanied Federal or Classical Revival houses. In Charleston, South Carolina, William Blacklock's square brick garden house, with Gothic-

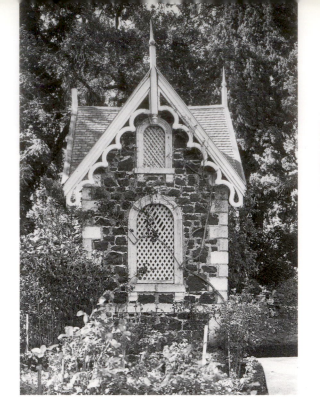

style windows and a matching carriage house, was built as early as 1800. A beautifully detailed Gothic gazebo dating to the 1840s backed the garden wall at 31 Meeting Street. More typical was the hexagonal summerhouse with concave roof ornamented with a scalloped frieze at 14 Legare Street.

In Natchez, Mississippi, the splendid suburban villa with encircling colonnade built in 1856 by Charles and Mary Dahlgren had Gothic Revival dependencies. A stone greenhouse was given a crenelated parapet and the brick poultry house was surmounted by an elaborate three-tiered dovecote.[33]

The Gothic followed settlers as far as California. In the 1840s William Davis Howard, a recent arrival from Massachusetts, ordered from Boston a prefabricated gingerbread cottage which he had shipped and erected in San Mateo. By the 1870s, the well-traveled owner of Howard's former property, Henry Pike Bowie (who had married Howard's widow), wanted "a landscape similar to those seen in Europe" and hired newly arrived Scots gardener John McLaren to create it.[34] McLaren's diary entries of his improvements allow a glimpse of the original garden. There was a mound between the house and the grapery which McLaren removed for "a more open and expansive experience." He noted that he had "eliminated all the flower borders except the Straight Border from the lath house toward the wood so the lawn extends from the house to the grove without a break."[35] A necessary feature of this garden was a water tower, which McLaren sought to hide in a pine grove.

LEFT: Garden house at "Temelec Hall," Sonoma, California. Photograph by Jack E. Boucher, 1960. Library of Congress, Historic American Buildings Survey, Washington, D.C. *Granville P. Swift built "Temelec Hall" in 1858 in the Classical Revival style, but his summerhouse combined Gothic details and proportions with arched window and door openings.*

Enoch Robinson. Octagonal summerhouse and rustic bench, Somerville, Massachusetts. Photograph by Edwin N. Peabody, c. 1880. Society for the Preservation of New England Antiquities, Boston
Robinson, who built himself a circular house with crenelated parapets in 1856, had probably read Fowler's A Home for All. *Robinson's tiny garden included a hexagonal garden house, a homemade rustic bench, and two cast-iron urns on pedestals.*

William M. Hunt's studio,
Magnolia, Massachusetts.
Edwin N. Peabody, c. 1880.
Society for the Preservation
of New England Antiquities,
Boston

BELOW: Cast-iron birdhouse.
c. 1860. 11 x 15 in. William
Doyle Galleries, New York
*By the 1840s, garden furniture
made in the new technology of
cast iron was readily available
in America. Included in some
manufacturers' catalogues
were birdhouses masquerading
as miniature villas in the popular Gothic, Queen Anne, or
Tuscan styles.*

Other California gardens made a merit of their water towers. At "Arbor Villa" in East Oakland, an octagonal wooden structure served both for water storage and as an observation platform from which to view the garden furnished with a grape arbor, glass house, fountain, lily pond, and rustic benches.[36]

PICTURESQUE PERCHES Prefabrication was the norm in California, in the midst of a building boom following the discovery of gold there. Most of the prefabs originated in New England, but in the 1850s Count Leonetto Cipriani had a house shipped in pieces from his native Italy for construction on the San Francisco peninsula. His farm and garden buildings were built locally, however, and included a prospect tower reminiscent of an Italian campanile.

A rustic prospect tower had been a feature of André Parmentier's noted nursery on Long Island in the 1830s. Praised by Downing and illustrated in the *Treatise,* it joined the long line of such picturesque garden lookouts, either freestanding or attached to trees, that ranged from Daniel Wadsworth's wooden tower at "Montevideo" to ephemeral treehouses. Among these was the fanciful perch-on-a-pole not unlike a birdhouse that noted Boston painter William Morris Hunt appended to his studio in Magnolia, Massachusetts.

Birdhouses were the repositories for all sorts of romantic architectural fantasies and appeared crowning summerhouses and other outbuildings as well as perched on poles. Hollis Hunnewell's amazing topiary garden in Wellesley, Massachusetts, for example, included a rustic octagonal summerhouse topped with an octagonal three-story miniature of itself to house a number of very fortunate birds.

Beginning in 1865 entrepreneur Joseph S. Potter embellished a vacant three-acre lot near his home in Arlington, Massachusetts, with an assortment of plantings and ornaments, among them a birdhouse said to represent his own dream house, never built. A three-story hexagonal wooden tower gave a bird's-eye view of the garden. Potter encouraged townsfolk to visit and enjoy "Potter's Grove" as he did himself; one of the many contemporary photographs of the garden shows Potter and his family enjoying tea on an elaborately set table there.[37]

There's a garden of dreams, where the crepe myrtle swings,
And the roses are white in the gloaming,
Where the hush of old beauty lies heavy and sweet,
Scarce stirred by the winds that are roaming . . . .

There time holds its breath, there shrubs grow to trees,
There beauty grows old in its questing,
And the garden dreams on in its fragrance-hung calm,
Where even the shadows are resting.

ELIZABETH EGGLESTON, "AN OLD-FASHIONED GARDEN"

Domestic Nostalgia *and* Suburban Comfort, 1870–1900

An entrepreneurial spirit characterized the boom period in New England, the Midwest, and the West after the Civil War, with a brief downturn in 1873. The frantic pace of life at the time—trolley cars and railroads rather than horse-drawn carriages, huge industries replacing local and domestic manufacture, the exponential growth and crowding of cities and the spread of suburbs— gave rise to a host of neurological symptoms. The frequently diagnosed complaint of "neurasthenia" was seen to be the inevitable reaction to a highly industrialized urban culture; significantly, both agoraphobia and anorexia were classified as mental disorders in 1873.[1]

A new, Darwinian outlook encouraged rampant self-interest in both politics and business. The successful businessman became a popular literary protagonist, anatomized in *The Gilded Age: A Tale of Today* (1873), a collaborative effort of Mark Twain and Charles Dudley Warner, and by William Dean Howells in his novel *The Rise of Silas Lapham* (1884). Fortunes were made in railroads, shipping, and myriad industries. At the same time, particularly following the depression of 1893, multitudes of small businesses and farms failed and many previously independent men became wage laborers. Even so, a man's economic success was celebrated, and seen to be a community benefit.

Mansions for the Middle Class Many proud capitalists, small as well as large, chose to demonstrate their success in their houses and grounds. Gardens recalling those of Italian villas or French châteaus were preferred, and called for fountains, statuary, and ornamental ironwork of all sorts, as well as acres of

Winslow Homer (1836–1910). Girl Watering Plants. 1875. Watercolor on paper, 11¼ x 9 in. Private collection
Indoor gardening, made easier by the advent of central heating, was a popular pursuit; after midcentury,
brown glazed pots with attached saucers joined traditional unglazed pots to house tender plants.
This young woman has moved her collection outside for the summer.

greenhouse-raised annuals and regiments of trained gardeners. All of history was ransacked for architectural forms—as a critic in 1880 put it, "This year it is the English Gothic, the next is the reign of Queen Anne, the year after, the French Renaissance, or perhaps a mixture of every style, by way of being eccentric."[2] New building technology seemed to promise that anything was possible—the balloon frame and the jigsaw were mainstays in wooden construction, cast iron had replaced wrought iron, and structural steel was introduced in 1890.

Ostentatious architecture with a picturesque mix of massive forms and a proliferation of ornament proclaimed both wealth and solidity as did the new Italianate villa built in the early 1870s by Henry Dickinson that replaced the family's modest eighteenth-century house in Hatfield, Massachusetts. The villa's unfenced grounds stretching along the road frontage were ornamented with evergreens planted in strict rows, meandering paths, urns, and a large octagonal summerhouse enclosed with lattice.[3]

A four-story mansion combining Second Empire elements with a classically columned porch was built about the same time by Milton S. Latham in San Francisco. The garden, enclosed in a cast-iron fence, featured a three-tiered iron fountain, numerous urns, and densely planted groves of trees. One of these circular plantings may have shel-

Gazebo at "Pitts Folly," Union-
town, Alabama. Photograph,
c. 1934–46. Library of Congress,
Historic American Buildings
Survey, Washington, D.C.
*This sort of open-lath summer-
house appeared all across the
country.*

tered a wooden lath garden pavilion like that at "Spottswoode" in St. Helena, California, where the rampant growth of the encircling linden trees
caused the pavilion's eventual demise. ("Spottswoode" was landscaped in
the picturesque style in the 1880s and many of the magnificent trees sur-
vive to this day.[4])

In Spartanburg, South Carolina, John Bomar Cleveland built an
imposing brick house in the Second Empire style and laid out a formal garden in 1884. The unfenced grounds of "Bonhaven," ornamented with flowering trees and shrubs, included an arched brick well house with pyramidal
roof and a rectangular garden house terminating one of three paths radiating from a sundial.[5]

Palm Beach, Florida, known today for its grand houses, was a frontier settlement as late as the 1870s. One of the early homesteads there was bought as a winter residence in 1886 by Denver businessman Robert R. McCormick, who expanded the house
and laid out an extensive garden that included two hexagonal pavilions. The grounds
were described in the local newspaper just before McCormick's "Seagull Cottage" was
bought by hotel magnate Henry Flagler. A row of coconut palms led up to the house,

F. A. Brader. RESIDENCE OF
JOSEPH AND SUSAN BOWMAN,
PERRY TP. STARK CO. OHIO.
1891. Pencil on paper, 37 x 50 in.
Private collection
*The fenced garden to the side of
the house combined vegetables
with flowers in neat beds; a
modest garden house or privy
occupied one corner.*

with three large flower beds for caladiums on either side. Numerous "secluded and circuitous paths" led to a fountain surrounded by crotons and geometric flower beds of
annuals, including one of "a crescent enclosing a star."[6]

In time, such architectural and horticultural excesses created a countercurrent,
a revulsion against meaningless ornament, overdecorated houses, and pretentious gardens. As an 1894 editorial in *Garden and Forest* put it: "By vulgar we mean ostentatious,
inappropriate, inartistic and ugly. We mean that most of our country places, large and
small, look as though the aim had been to spend as much money in them as possible, and
to make as much show as possible for that amount of money."[7]

Many thoughtful Americans sought alternatives to shoddy, mass-produced goods,
homes built for display rather than comfort, and gardens filled with meaningless beds of
labor-intensive annuals. The Aesthetic Movement, and a new interest in America's colonial past encouraged by the centennial in 1876 (culminating after 1900 in a full-blown
Colonial Revival), offered attractive possibilities.

THE AESTHETIC MOVEMENT AND THE OLD-FASHIONED GARDEN

The Aesthetic Movement, originating in England and spread
through the writings of John Ruskin and William Morris, reached a wide audience in
America through the decorative arts shown at the 1876 Philadelphia Centennial Exposition, where the era of the nation's birth was celebrated. The movement's espousal of

Edward Lamston Henry (1841–1919). IN THE GARDEN. c. 1890. Oil on board, 9¾ x 14 in. Alexander Gallery, New York
As settings for his nostalgic evocations of bygone times, genre painter E. L. Henry used his own house and garden and those of his neighbors in Cragsmoor, New York.

handcrafted objects with graceful shapes and decorative patterns of color and line provided compelling alternatives to the mediocrity of mass-produced goods.

In this country, the restrained elegance of eighteenth-century American design was seen as a better model for emulation than any foreign style. Influential critic Clarence Cook, an apologist for the Aesthetic Movement, in a series of essays on decoration in *Scribner's Magazine* (published as *The House Beautiful* in 1877), hailed the new interest in colonial design as "one of the best signs of returning good taste in a community that has long been the victim to the whims and impositions of foreign fashions."[8] He led a democratic revolution in home decoration aimed at comfort and charm and proposed an all-purpose, informal "living room" for the seldom used, formal parlor.

The Aesthetic Movement encouraged a studied informality in both gardens and interior decoration as the garden itself began to be viewed as an outdoor living space.

Rigid geometric beds of annuals were considered tasteless, and American gardening books began to espouse informal old-fashioned perennial gardens modeled on colonial ones. Among the first of these books was Anna Bartlett Warner's *Gardening by Myself* (1872), noteworthy for its engaging first-person voice, its sensible advice, and for its encouragement of women to do heavy gardening work themselves. Art critic Mariana Van Rensselaer's *Art Out-of-Doors* (1893) was more theoretical, and perhaps the most influential among aesthetically sophisticated gardeners.

While early American gardens were an inspiration for many amateur gardeners, those who were well read and well traveled were aware of changing gardening ideas abroad. Noted gardener Anna Gilman Hill wrote that her mother at "Niederhurst," Sneden's Landing, New York, had a comprehensive gardening library that included the 1881 edition of English horticulturist William Robinson's *The Wild Garden*. She recalled that, having read the book, "My mother discarded her carpet-bedding at once" even though "all the trained gardeners would have nothing to do with this new helter-skelter mode of planting."[9]

A CALIFORNIA GARDEN The idea of the old-fashioned garden originated in New England, but the traditional perennial garden that inspired it could be found all across the country. The gold rush of 1849 lured thousands of young men from overcrowded New England farms, including several Bixby brothers and cousins from Somerset County, Maine. In 1853, Llewellyn Bixby and two of his cousins bought Rancho San Justo, located near San Juan Bautista in the San Benito Valley of Southern California, and embarked on lucrative careers as sheep farmers. The house the partners built to accommodate their young families, though adobe, was painted white with green shutters with a steeply gabled roof ornamented with gingerbread edging. The flower garden in front of the house was enclosed by a white picket fence and filled with perennials familiar to the newly transplanted Yankees.[10]

Rancho Los Cerritos, now part of Los Angeles, became part of the Bixby holdings in 1866. Here there was an existing grand adobe house with extending wings. The two-acre garden was overlooked by the veranda that stretched across the back of the house, and was enclosed by the house wings and a high wall. Even this very Spanish enclosure had in the 1870s and 1880s echoes of the old-fashioned garden, as described by Llewellyn Bixby's daughter. "It was laid out in three tiers of four beds, each about fifty feet square, with a wide border about the whole. They were separated by walks, edged with brick. Near the house were flowers and shrubs, but further away grapes were plant-

Sallie Cover. HOMESTEAD OF
ELLSWORTH L. BALL, GARFIELD
COUNTY, NEBRASKA. c. 1880–90.
Oil on canvas, 19½ x 23 in.
Nebraska State Historical
Society, Lincoln
*Sallie Cover was a farmwife who
recorded the efforts put toward
creating a garden and orchard
around her neighbor's sod house.*

ed, and oranges, pomegranates, and figs. At the end of the rose-shaded path leading from
the front door stood a summer house, bowered in the white-blossomed Madeira vine and
set in a thick bed of the blue-flowered periwinkle...."[11]

ARBORS, TRELLISES, AND VINES Ella Rodman Church,
a novelist and writer on home decoration, advised on garden layouts and furnishings in
The Home Garden (1881). Here she argued that "The patterns usually given in works on
horticulture are often more suitable for embroidery or mosaic-work.... a garden made
on these principles has a bare, dreary look...." Instead she advocated perennial gardens
with "old-fashioned arbors and arches covered with roses, or clematis, honeysuckle and
Virginia creeper."[12] General-interest publications as well as gardening magazines took
up the theme of the old-fashioned garden of box-bordered perennial beds furnished with
traditional arbors, trellises, and summerhouses.[13]

In some gardens, these traditional structures took on new identities and sometimes bizarre forms. In the 1880s at "Westlawn," Washington, Connecticut, a teahouse

was made by inserting an octagonal lath-roofed summerhouse, crowned with a wooden teapot finial, into the center of an arched and latticed arbor.

The old-fashioned garden was seen as an extension of the house, which was to sit snugly in its grounds rather than dominate its surroundings. As a writer in *Garden and Forest* put it, "by vine and herbage, flower and fruit, the dwelling is made to seem a growth rather than a construction . . . hardness of contrast is banished, and sharpness of outline toned into agreeable mystery, and true picturesque effect obtained."[14] Trellises for vines or roses were added to even the most modest dwellings from the southern tenant farmer's cabin to the sod house on the frontier. Arched trellises often circled the doorway of the house or framed the garden entrance.

Vine-covered cottages like that of John Austen on Staten Island, New York, visible from the steamboats plying the Hudson River, were much admired. Austen wrote to his family in 1874 that a passenger on one boat had related that "he was so charmed with the looks of a long low house on Staten Island all mantled in vines. He said all the passengers were admiring our house and talking about it."[15]

Julian Alden Weir (1852–1919).
THE GREY TRELLIS. 1891.
Oil on canvas, 26 x 21½ in.
Collection Mr. and Mrs.
Willard G. Clark
*Painter Julian Alden Weir's
farm in Branchville, Connecticut,
had an enclosed flower garden
entered through two rustic arbors,
and the paling-fenced vegetable
garden seen here.*

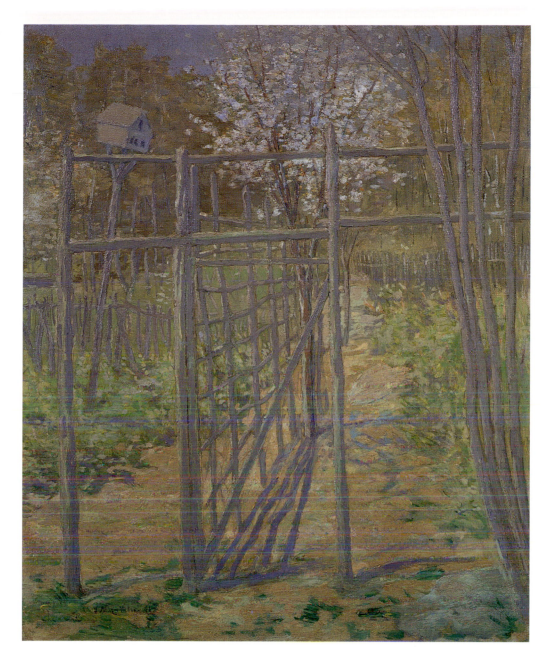

"HOME SWEET HOME" Vine-covered cottages were
admired for more than their charm—they represented a refuge from the economic and
social turmoil of the time. The rural past and its simpler way of life were idealized at the
very moment that, throughout much of New England, farms were being abandoned as
the railroad made cheap produce from the Midwest available on the East Coast. While
this provided an opportunity for those in the affluent middle class to acquire a summer

F. A. Brader. John V. R. Evans Farm, Spring Town, Berks Co. Penna. 1881. Pencil on paper, 30 x 49 in. Private collection
The Evans farm had a decorative circular flower bed in the enclosed front yard as well as a fenced garden to the side, divided into four large squares. A neat privy topped by a birdhouse stood beyond the fence.

home, it was disquieting to many. J. B. Harrison in his article "The Abandoned Farms of New Hampshire" lamented that "the truth is that the old New England civilization and organization of society has here mostly come to an end."[16] John Howard Payne's sentimental song "Home Sweet Home," eulogizing his boyhood dwelling, an eighteenth-century saltbox in East Hampton, Long Island, became a leitmotif of the longing for a vanished pastoral America.

Both the decorative artists of the Aesthetic Movement and those seeking to preserve the traditional values of an earlier, more civil America focused on the home. The home and its grounds were believed to inculcate old-fashioned values as well as furnishing aesthetically pleasing surroundings. As the well-known textile designer Candace Wheeler wrote in 1893, "A perfectly furnished house is a crystallization of the culture, the habits, and the taste of the family, and not only expresses but *makes* character."[17]

In the 1870s and 1880s the proliferation of publications focusing on the home and garden, mostly aimed at women, provided opportunities for many women to forge careers as authors and journalists. Among the most prolific was Mary Virginia Terhune, who, beginning as novelist "Marion Harland," went on to write scores of books on housekeeping, etiquette, and colonial homes.

For such writers, both domesticity and familiarity with the home life of America's founding fathers were seen as strategies

Below: Garden gate, Ohio. c. 1870. Walnut, 60 x 53 in. Collection Mr. and Mrs. Jerome Blum
Picket gates lent themselves to elaborate variations. Suggestions could be found in manuals such as George Martin's, Fences, Gates and Bridges (1887).

Noyes summerhouse,
Cambridge, Massachusetts.
Photograph, 1902. Society for
the Preservation of New
England Antiquities, Boston
*Both the Noyes summerhouse
and main house were in the
Colonial Revival style. On the
back of the photograph it was
noted that the birdhouse had been
"made by Penelope at school."*

to inculcate patriotism and traditional values in a rootless immigrant population with no knowledge of the nation's past. America's historic preservation movement had its origins in the restoration of homes of significant figures in American history who were seen to embody traditional virtues and values. George Washington's "Mount Vernon" was the first in 1860, and by 1895 there were twenty historic houses open to the public.[18]

Popular historian Alice Morse Earle's *Home Life in Colonial Days* (1898), which documented the daily life of ordinary people through household objects, incorporated as its last chapter her article on "Old Time Flower Gardens" that had appeared in *Scribner's Magazine* in 1896. Underlying the book was the belief that association with old-fashioned gardens and their long-cultivated plants as well as with handcrafted objects from America's past could ameliorate the incivilities and discomforts of the modern world as well as communicate the virtues of a simpler and more dignified way of life.

Earle wrote not only of plants but of structures in the garden. "What cheerful and appropriate furnishings the old-time gardens had; benches full of straw bee-skepes and wooden beehives . . .; frequently also a well filled dovecote. Sometimes was seen a sun-dial. . . . At the edge of the farm garden often stood the well-sweep, one of the most picturesque adjuncts of the country door yard. Its successor, the roofed well with bucket, stone and chain . . . had a certain appropriateness as part of the garden furnishings."[19]

As members of old families or those newly arrived in the middle class built new houses, they often chose plans that reflected American colonial prototypes, and decorated their gardens with traditional structures. The James A. Noyes house in Cambridge, Massachusetts, designed by the Boston firm of Longfellow, Alden and Harlow in 1883, had a gambrel roof and Federal detailing. Its garden was amply furnished with an assortment of benches, chairs, and tables, a seesaw and swing, and an octagonal summerhouse with bell roof that recalled ones of a century earlier.

FOR THE BIRDS

For novelist and nature writer Mabel Osgood Wright, patriotism, wild bird protection, and the old-fashioned garden were intimately connected. Wright had grown up in New York City and had spent summers in Fairfield, Connecticut, at "Waldstein," the home built in 1858 by her father, the Reverend Samuel Osgood. The grounds included a delightful rustic summerhouse, from which the Reverend Osgood delivered extempore sermons, as well as a woodland garden and extensive flower beds. After her father's death, Wright and her husband occupied the house during the summer months. Her deliberately old-fashioned garden was the fictionalized setting of a series of garden "romances," beginning with *The Garden of a Commuter's Wife* (1901).

Much of Wright's first book, *The Friendship of Nature: A New England Chronicle of Birds and Flowers* (1894), had appeared as articles in the *New York Times* written while she studied with ornithologist Frank Chapman. The book's popularity led to a commission from Macmillan for the well-respected bird manual *Birdcraft, a Field Book of Two Hundred Song, Game and Water Birds* (1895), which was followed by *Citizen Bird* (1897).

The Audubon movement, begun with the aim of wild bird protection, in the 1890s espoused the nativist and patriotic sentiments held by many of its members. Wright, for example, believed that civic virtue and a sense of community were largely derived from one's colonial ancestry.

In helping to found the Connecticut Audubon Society in 1898, she drew on the membership of the Fairfield chapter of the Daughters of the American Revolution, of which she had been an original member. (The Fairfield chapter of The Garden Club of America that Wright helped found likewise drew on the DAR membership.) Wright was elected first president of the Society in 1898 and served for twenty-five years. In 1915 she established the Birdcraft Sanctuary, the first private bird sanctuary in the nation.[20]

The Audubon Society urged building birdhouses, as did other organizations. The Massachusetts State Grange, for example, published pamphlets on attracting wild birds and building birdhouses, baths, and feeders. As might be expected in such a bird-conscious era, extravagant birdhouses appeared all across the country. In 1887 young Frank Schuster built a turreted mansion for birds that adorned a pole in the Leesburg, Virginia, garden of his grandparents. It was later moved to the roof of a rustic cedar summerhouse that he had also constructed there.[21]

RUSTIC WORK Many magazines gave instructions for constructing rustic arbors, trellises, summerhouses, and birdhouses for the garden, beginning at midcentury with a group of articles in *The Horticulturist*. The writer of an article on "Hints and Designs for Rustic Buildings" felt that "the more humble and simple

cottage grounds . . . and the modest garden of the suburban amateur" ought to be embellished with "seats, bowers, grottoes and arbors, of rustic work. . . ." In 1850 "An Amateur" recommended rustic seats, boxes and baskets for flowers, and rustic arbors to be built of red cedar.[22]

Homemade rustic baskets holding vines and bright annuals substituted for more expensive cast-iron urns in many front yards, inspired by articles such as "Rustic Work for the Lawn" in *American Gardening*. Wooden boxes were to be covered with bark strips and set on twig legs; open-work twig stands or bark-covered baskets were other suggestions, all "simply constructed and inexpensive as well as artistic."[23] An article on "The Rustic Touch in the Garden" in *The Ladies' Home Journal* illustrated arbors, arches, summerhouses, and bridges, and even a Japanese-influenced pavilion perched high in a tree in a California garden.[24]

Rustic summerhouses and arbors decorated large as well as small gardens. The three-acre property in Springfield, Massachusetts, where Edward Brewer built a house designed by Calvert Vaux in 1863, boasted hundreds of roses, specimen trees, and a circular rustic summerhouse with tiny Gothic stained-glass windows.[25] By century's end, there were firms specializing in such work across the country. The Rustic Construction Company in New York City advertised widely that it could provide rustic arbors, seats, tables, gateways, birdhouses, planters, summerhouses, and even bridges.

The relatively modest homes and gardens of well-known figures like naturalist and writer John Burroughs served as exemplars of proper aesthetic choices. Burroughs was visited at his home "Riverby," West Park, New York, by a writer for *American Gar-*

dening who found the house "wrapped in a golden robe of vines." Burroughs's study by the Hudson River, "a bark-covered little building," stood near a rustic summerhouse that was "open in front to a magnificent view of the flowing river and the distant hills."[26]

MARK TWAIN'S STUDY

A more architecturally sophisticated study was built in 1874 for Samuel Clemens (Mark Twain) by his sister-in-law in the garden of the Langdon family's "Quarry Farm" outside Elmira, New York, where Clemens, his wife, Olivia Langdon, and children spent the summer. He wrote delightedly to a friend, "It

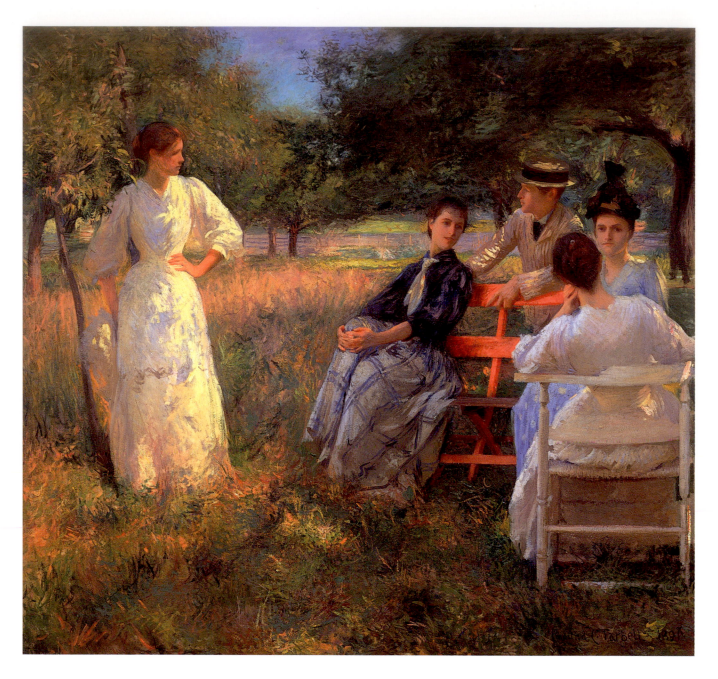

Edmund Charles Tarbell (1862–1938). IN THE ORCHARD. 1891. Oil on canvas, 60¾ x 65½ in.
Courtesy Terra Museum of American Art, Chicago. Daniel J. Terra Collection (1.1992)
From the 1860s onward, women as well as men enjoyed outdoor leisure sports such as croquet and tennis.
Socialization was encouraged by such a grouping of chairs and benches, often castoffs from the house, painted in bright colors.

Robert Blum (1857–1903). Two Idlers. 1888. Oil on canvas, 29 x 40 in. The National Academy Museum and School of Fine Arts, New York
Impressionist Robert Blum painted his friends William and Laura Baer on their porch in Brick Church, New Jersey, surrounded by symbols of leisure: a hammock, a wicker chair, and a bamboo table for a paperback novel, cigarettes, and a pitcher of lemonade.

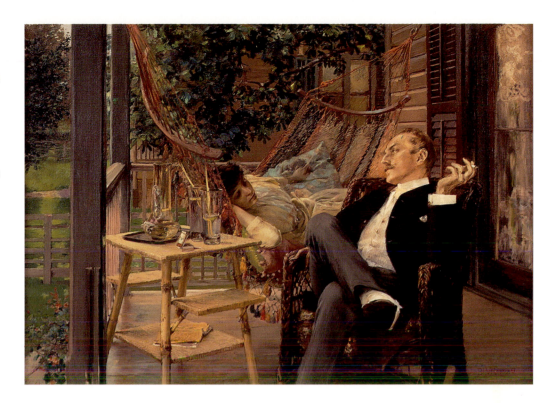

is the loveliest study you ever saw. It is octagonal, with a peaked roof, each face filled with a spacious window, and it sits perched in complete isolation on the top of an elevation that commands leagues of valley and city and retreating ranges of distant blue hills."[27] Here he began *Tom Sawyer,* writing as many as fifty pages a day in an illusory isolation that was only a stone's throw from the house.

Work had begun on the Clemenses new Tudor-style home in Hartford, Connecticut, the previous year and they were able to move in following the summer at "Quarry Farm." While certainly not simple, the house was praised by all their literary friends for its charm and the "homelike" qualities so important at the time. A notable feature was the semicircular conservatory, a design invented by neighbor Harriet Beecher Stowe. Its effect was that of a summerhouse turned inside out, as described by writer William Dean Howells after a visit. "The plants were set into the ground, and the flowering vines climbed up the sides and overhung the roof above the silent spray of the fountain. . . ."[28] By 1874 Mark Twain had become a literary lion and his house a magnet for sightseers. Private retreats like Twain's conservatory and the vine-covered veranda at the back of his house were found in homes of those less famous who also valued such protected yet out-of-door living areas.

FLOATING SUMMERHOUSES Harriet Prescott Spofford, who wrote Gothic novels in the 1860s, in the 1890s produced stories set in New England, a change in focus from the sublime and romantic to the domestic and local that occurred in so many aspects of American culture. On an island near Newburyport, Massachusetts, in 1874 she built a rustic thatched-roof summerhouse that projected into the water like a tethered boat. The garden surrounding her new gambrel-roof house was entered through a rustic gate set into a wall of massive stones.

If Spofford's summerhouse only appeared to float, others actually did so. Artist and craftsman Charles Frederic Eaton's floating, open-sided barge with a Japanese roof was probably constructed for the Eatons' Venetian Fête in July 1893 on their estate "Riso Rivo" in Montecito, California. Seemingly self-propelled, it was guided across the small lake along a concealed underwater cable. Garden writer Phebe Humphreys described it as "a pavilion boat built in the form of a floating tea room—a square structure, with a picturesque roof of yellow thatch, and broad overhanging eaves" decorated with flower boxes filled with vines which twined up to ornament the thatched roof.[29]

BENCHES AND SEATS A tremendous variety of ready-made garden furniture became available after the Civil War. Cast iron was offered by American foundries in thousands of patterns while manufacturers of wooden furniture produced folding canvas chairs, steamer chairs, hammocks, and slat furniture of all descriptions. The F. H. Earl Manufacturing Company in Plano, Illinois, for example, boasted in its 1904 catalogue of *Ladders, Lawn Swings, Lawn Furniture, Wheelbarrows*, that it had sold more than 100,000 lawn swings in the previous five years. Photographs of gardens show all of these in use, along with homemade furniture and worn wooden chairs, tables, and benches, retired from the house and given a coat of paint for porch and yard duty.

Bright colors were preferred for wooden seats—startling greens, blues, even orange. Margaret Boyd recalled a garden party in Marin County, California, to celebrate her sixteenth birthday in 1886. "The only disturbing event was that the garden benches freshly painted with the brightest of green paint for the occasion were not quite dry and several young ladies went home with their dainty organdy dresses crossbarred with green."[30]

American Impressionists showed a fondness for orange, not only in their paintings but in their garden furniture. Edmund Tarbell included an orange bench in a painting of 1891. Hamilton Hamilton in his *Summer, Campobello* (1900) depicted an old Boston rocker painted orange for outdoor use. Irving Wiles, who gardened in New York State,

Harriet Prescott Spofford. Summerhouse from the bridge, Newburyport, Massachusetts. Photograph by George Noyes, c. 1890. Society for the Preservation of New England Antiquities, Boston

showed an orange Boston rocker in *On the Terrace* (1887) and included an orange bench in *Mrs. Wiles in the Garden*.

When artist Frank Benson bought an old farm in New Hampshire in 1904, one of his first improvements was a roofless piazza across the front of the house furnished with a green-painted bench built by himself. Visible from the piazza was an extensive perennial garden begun by Benson's wife, Ellen, where, her granddaughter recalled, "Great drifts of colors blended and complemented each other beautifully."[31] As the Colonial Revival gained momentum, white became the preferred color for garden furnishings—in Benson's later paintings done of the piazza, the bench is white.

THE SUNKEN GARDEN. WISCASSET, ME.

The simple old white houses of New England are classics quite as truly as any Grecian temple — and in the midst of their prim, old, box-bordered little gardens, they present far saner and safer models for us generally, than those which many are too prone to follow.

GRACE TABOR, THE LANDSCAPE GARDENING BOOK, 1911

ARTS *and* CRAFTS *and the* COLONIAL REVIVAL, 1900–1930

At the World's Columbian Exposition of 1893 in Chicago and the 1904 Louisiana Purchase Exposition in St. Louis, many of the state pavilions were reproductions of historic American buildings. Their influence was far-reaching: during the next few decades, the colonial style proliferated in architecture, interior decoration, and gardens. The embroilment of Europe in World War I reinforced America's distaste for imported European styles. Emerging from the war as a world power, America embraced the colonial style as a national symbol.

As a writer in the *White Pines Series of Architectural Monographs* proclaimed in 1916, "Colonial is our national style of Architecture."[1] Its use in house and garden signified both good taste and affiliation with long-established families. The Arts and Crafts movement provided modern design alternatives, and in California and the Southwest the vernacular adobe and the bungalow were adopted as particularly American forms.

Many of the shelter magazines founded at this time espoused both colonial and Arts and Crafts designs. *House and Garden* was begun in 1901 by three Philadelphia architects who worked in the Colonial Revival Style. Wilson Eyre, the editor for the first four years, also promoted the Arts and Crafts movement, as did Gustav Stickley in his *Craftsman* magazine founded the same year. Other popular magazines—among them the upmarket *Country Life in America,* also begun in 1901, and *Suburban Life,* started in 1905— reflected the interests of those members of the middle class who had fled to the surburbs or who had second homes in rural areas made accessible by the advent of the automobile.

Both the advocates of Colonial Revival design and those who espoused Arts and Crafts ideology were united in their disgust for conspicuous consumption, their rever-

"The Sunken Garden, Wiscasset, Me." Postcard, 1917. Collection the author
*This garden had many of the objects found in the old-fashioned garden:
an arched trellis, birdhouse, birdbath, and enclosing walls.*

ence for handcraftsmanship, and their preference for indigenous forms. California poet Charles Keeler's *The Simple Home* (1904), a plea for small houses untrammeled by mass-produced objects and ornaments, and for distinctive gardens "sequestered from public view, forming a room walled with growing things," articulated the aesthetic ideals of many members of the middle class fed up with consumerism. The book's title may refer to a popular polemic of the day, *The Simple Life* (1904), by French writer Charles Wagner, who lamented, "Our eyes are wounded by the crying spectacle of gaudy ornament, venal art, and senseless and graceless luxury. Wealth coupled with bad taste sometimes makes us regret that so much money is in circulation to provoke the creation of such a prodigality of horrors."[2]

THE OLD FARMHOUSE Old houses, relics of a vanished America, had become newly desirable both as summer homes and permanent residences. Among hundreds of books published about all aspects of country life were many on remodeling old houses. Mary H. Northend, a writer and photographer from Salem, Massachusetts, known for her books on colonial houses and their history, pointed out the "wealth of possibilities" in her *Remodeled Farmhouses* (1915). Not the least of the appeal of these old dwellings for Northend was their associations; they had "sheltered the most ardent patriots of our land, men whose gallant deeds have made them famous. . . ."[3]

For Northend, the addition of a piazza or porch, imperative in remodeling, presented something of a problem for there was no colonial authority for it. Nonetheless, her photographs show pergolas added to terraces for a sort of "pergola porch," with grapevines trained over it for shade. She considered the proper garden for such a house to be an old-fashioned one enclosed in a white picket fence. Her next book, *Garden Ornaments* (1916), illustrated more modern pergolas as well as traditional garden structures.

These piazzas were meant to be used, and they were. Painter Susan Hale spent long summers in Matunuck, Rhode Island, where the house had several piazzas. According to her brother, Edward Everett Hale, "She would breakfast on the piazza . . . . In the afternoon she took to the east piazza . . . for afternoon tea. She often went off for a stroll in the late afternoon, and after supper finished the day by a short time on the front piazza."[4]

Charles Edward Hooper, who wrote frequently on architecture and decoration for *Country Life in America*, in his *Reclaiming the Old*

Stars and bars garden gate, Maine. Early twentieth century. Poplar, 86 x 67 in. American Primitive Gallery, New York
This sort of picket gate that one can see through, a vernacular clair voyée, has been popular since the beginning of the century.

Edward Lamston Henry.
THE HUCKSTER. 1914. Oil on
canvas, 13¾ x 23½ in. Richard
York Gallery, New York
*The gazebo was sited to take
advantage of the spectacular view
from the cliffs at Cragsmoor, New
York, where this was painted.
The covered trellis gate became a
popular garden ornament at the
turn of the century.*

House (1913) included a chapter on gardens. For these old homes he suggested enclosed flower gardens arranged in geometric beds. Traditional arches, arbors, and trellises, latticed summerhouses, and appropriate outbuildings such as privies and icehouses were to be located on an axis in relation to the house.

Frequent magazine articles popularized such gardens. An article on "Quaint Beauty in Old-Time Gardens" in *Better Homes and Gardens*, for example, included a typical illustration of an old-fashioned garden enclosed by a rose-covered fence and entered through an arched gateway. A writer by 1924 could state, "The New England flower garden has become a national institution.... We need—no less today than did our ancestors in the years gone by—the decorative note of peace which the lovely gardens gave to the surroundings of those white, homelike houses."[5]

AN OLD-FASHIONED GARDEN   In 1905, Julia Cummins and her husband joined the growing ranks of young families who rented or bought summer homes in the country. The Cumminses eighteenth-century house on twenty-five acres of meadow and woods was in the foothills of the Adirondacks, easily accessible by railway and a carriage ride. One of their first improvements was white paint

for the house and green shutters for the windows. A flagstone terrace and pergola were added so that the house seemed to "spread out in all directions . . . to fit down on the land."[6]

Julia Cummins began her garden when, as she confided in her account of its making, *My Garden Comes of Age* (1926), "I was aroused to envy by the lovely old-fashioned flower borders of a neighbor. There Hollyhocks bloomed to perfection and masses of Sweet William, Bergamot, Cockscomb and many brilliant annuals." Like many other beginning gardeners, Cummins was unaware of the scores of garden books then in print. She wrote, "I was curiously ignorant of any such literature and had seen but few good gardens when I started my own."[7]

Her ideas of the "gracious and the beautiful" in home and garden were formed by the pervasive idealization of early American design. She wrote, "As we think of the dignity of the early Colonial houses of New England, and the spacious elegance of the same period of Southern architecture with its box-bordered gardens, we realize that since that time we have passed through an era of bad taste in both houses and gardens."[8] Thus she centered her rose garden, entered through an arched trellis painted white, on a sundial. Her flower beds, bordering a long walk from the house to the woods, were edged with planks and filled with old-fashioned flowers.

FENCES AND WALLS Frank Scott's influential *The Art of Beautifying Suburban Home Grounds* (1870) had called for eliminating front fences so that adjacent lawns could be seen as one. As laws requiring that animals be kept enclosed became the norm, many homeowners followed his advice. By 1900 there was a reaction. As Alice Morse Earle pointed out in her *Old Time Gardens* (1901), a growing appreciation of early walled gardens like those in Germantown, Pennsylvania, or Salem, Massachusetts, called into question "the modern fashion in American towns of pulling down walls and fences, removing the boundaries of lawns, and living in full view of every passer-by, in a public grassy park . . ."[9] A decade later, a writer for *House and Garden* could report that "The garden is no longer between the house and the road, but behind or at the end, screened in some way from the automobile dust and the curious gaze of passers-by."[10] A green barrier was still preferable to an impenetrable wall, however. Jessie Frothingham, who named her own garden in Princeton, New Jersey, "Hortus Inclusus" (friendlier than *hortus conclusus*), wrote in 1913, "there is one advantage that fences and hedges have over walls—they do not irritate the public by a too conspicuous and candid desire to be private."[11]

Even Gustav Stickley's *Craftsman* magazine praised old enclosed gardens and their traditional furnishings. An article on the gardens of Salem pointed out that "they are not especially connected with the houses as is fashionable in modern landscape gardening by pergolas, peristyles or covered arches. . . . Sometimes they are entered by a demure little white gate, again an arbor leads the way into their center. In almost every case they are enclosed at their outer boundaries by a fence."[12]

California architect Irving J. Gill, in an article in *Craftsman* on "The Home of the Future," cited the colonial houses of New England, the stone farmhouses of the mid-Atlantic states, and the adobe for their simplicity and fitness. He saw the Mission style as particularly appropriate for California, however, and the enclosed court in old private houses like the Casa de Estudillo (known as "Ramona's house" after the heroine of Helen Hunt Jackson's bestselling 1884 novel) ideal for outdoor living. The arched porticos of the house formed three sides of the court, and a high wall backed with a grape arbor, the fourth. In such an enclosure "There was always a sheltered and a sunny side, always seclusion and an outlook into the garden."[13]

THE BUNGALOW Gustav Stickley wrote in the *Craftsman* magazine that "the most desirable thing one can have in the way of a home is an old house built by one's grandfather or great-grandfather. . . . " The next best for Stickley was a Craftsman-built house. Such a home was designed by architect Wade Pipes for his

A California Residence in Winter.

brother John in Portland, Oregon, in 1911. The garden was a notable one; it was described as being "laid out formally enough to provide the most effective opportunities for walks, planted rows and groups of shrubbery on an ordinary lot . . . It is a garden to live in and enjoy. . . ."[14]

The bungalow, a one-story house with a sheltering porch, available ready-to-assemble from many mail-order companies, provided an inexpensive alternative. The April 1910 issue of *Bungalow Magazine* (begun the previous year) featured a low five-room house, its lines continued by a pergola leading to the detached garage. A rustic summerhouse was the focus of a circular garden hidden behind the garage.[15]

Few actual bungalows had such carefully designed grounds; most were ornamented with the mass-produced trellises, arbors, and gates available across the country. Rustic summerhouses were a mainstay of companies furnishing garden structures, but were not universally admired. One writer on landscape design complained, "The 'rustic' treatment favoured by commercial makers of garden houses is not only expensive, but it is meaningless, inartistic, structurally unsound, and not durable."[16]

PERGOLAS Pergolas were ubiquitous in most gardens, whether inspired by the Colonial Revival or the Arts and Crafts movement, and were equally at home in formal or informal settings. While the term was appropriated from

Abbott Fuller Graves
(1859–1936). SUMMER GARDEN
WALK. C. 1900. Oil on canvas,
12 x 9 in. Private collection
*Graves specialized in painting
old-fashioned gardens around
Kennebunk, Maine, such as this
one entered through a covered
gate.*

Italian gardens, the American pergola was seen to be a native development, an offshoot of the colonial arbor and was as at home in the Northeast as on the West Coast. As was pointed out in an article in *Craftsman* magazine, "Pergolas: The Most Picturesque and Practical Feature of the Modern Out-Door Life," the notion that the garden ought to be an extension of the living space encouraged such open and airy shelters, even in less-than-temperate locations.[17]

Numerous articles appeared instructing amateurs in the construction of all sorts of pergolas. Garden writer Grace Tabor's design for an "adaptable gated arbor" in *The American Home* was thirty-six feet in length. As she pointed out, "Sometimes as a uniting factor, sometimes as a dividing boundary, an arbor or pergola, or whatever you may call it, is an ever-ready help in unifying the garden scheme." A Wisconsin reader of *Better Homes and Gardens* reported building one after developing "pergola fever" as a result of articles "describing how some amateur . . . had built something for his garden which was an unqualified success."[18]

Pergolas ranged from the simple rustic one made by artist Robert Vonnoh as the gateway to the pond on his property in Old Lyme, Connecticut, to the elegant marble edifice erected by mural painter William de Leftwich Dodge at his "Villa Francesca" overlooking the sea on Long Island's North Shore. They could be enclosed with lattice for use as summerhouses as was the one built in 1917 for the Staiti garden in Houston, Texas. Typical was the one that enclosed two sides of a new garden begun in 1909 by

Grape arbor, Neosho, Missouri. Photograph by Ida Dougan, c. 1915. Collection Michael B. Dougan
Ida Dougan's garden was furnished with a wooden glider and wicker chairs. An architectural birdhouse on a pole rises above the vine-covered fence of the vegetable garden.

Adaline Thomson and described in *American Homes and Gardens*. The garden was laid out in four triangular beds filled with old-fashioned perennials and centered on a sundial. The pergola was made of logs with the bark left on, the cross pieces of smaller split logs. Despite its rustic construction, as Thomson related, it was "extremely artistic in effect," and gave "tone and dignity to the whole garden."[19]

THE GARDEN LIVING ROOM

A writer in *The American Home* described the expected structures in a garden of the 1920s: "Sundials impart an old-world character to a garden and add a touch of poetry. An arbor or a summerhouse provides a bit of grateful shade and privacy; trellises also when covered with the green of graceful vines." Equally essential for this writer, and others at the time, was the furnished outdoor living room. Another writer for the magazine suggested locations: "We may have it in the form of a flagstone terrace at our kitchen door with an awning stretched over it—if not an awning, a grape arbor. We may have it under an old apple tree. . . . Again we may group it around the shelter-seat at the far end of the garden path, it is not so much *where* we have it as *that* we have it."[20]

This outdoor living room was distinguished from earlier uses of the garden for entertaining by its informality and casual assemblage of convenient furnishings. Photographs of the time show wicker chairs and tables, steamer chairs, Adirondack chairs, wooden benches and stools, kitchen chairs, folding park chairs, and rustic seats mixed indiscriminately. Comfort and convenience rather than any preconceived notions of what was suitable seemed to be the only criteria. In inclement weather, the porch, now called

a veranda or piazza, was the locus of outdoor conviviality. Its furnishings might include "a hammock hung across one end, comfortable willow chairs, a folding table that will serve for a breakfast table, and a small table for a few books, magazines and papers."[21]

GARDEN ARCHITECTURE

During these decades, landscape architecture became a recognized profession that included many notable women practitioners. The views of both professionals and amateurs on the importance of garden structure and structures could be found in numerous books and articles aimed toward the home gardener as well as those able to hire landscape designers.

Landscape architect Ruth Dean wrote of the role of design in *The Livable House: Its Garden*. For her, architectural features such as arbors, gates, and walls were "not only important sources of interest in themselves, but the means of completing the garden . . . and giving it a finished appearance."[22] Included among the many photographs of gardens designed by landscape architects were four views of the garden made by amateur Anna Gilman Hill in East Hampton, Long Island. Enclosed in poured concrete walls pierced by arched doorways, it had for Dean "a delightfully spontaneous quality in its design—an unstudied simplicity which professional work is apt to lose. . . ."[23]

Hill revealed in her own engaging book *Forty Years of Gardening* (1938) that the idea for "Grey Gardens" had come from an illustration of an old walled garden in Pennsylvania. Inside the protecting walls she visualized "arches recessed in the walls for seats and a fountain . . . a thatched tool house just outside the far gate towards the vegetable garden and . . . an exedra overlooking the sea."[24]

Landscape architect Loring Underwood's *The Garden and Its Accessories* favored gardens modeled after Colonial ones, "good exponents of the proper use of simple garden accessories." In such a garden near the house, paths spanned by arches would radiate from a grape arbor with a summerhouse in one corner. One of the summerhouses

E. G. and Dorothy Walton in the garden at 802 Mount Curve Avenue, Minneapolis. Photograph by A. D. Roth, c. 1915. Minnesota Historical Society, Minneapolis

In this Minnesota garden an old tree stump was made into a flower basket with a wire handle, more wire and iron pipes formed a pointed arch trellis, and the summerhouse was screened and covered with a tin roof; a traditional sundial centered the flower beds.

illustrated was the rustic thatched one built by the author himself in his own garden.[25]

Amateur Phebe Westcott Humphreys's *The Practical Book of Garden Architecture* (1914) included all sorts of structures designed to be lived in, including tea pavilions, bathhouses, and several splendid tree houses, all very informal. In her chapter on "Dependable Bird Houses," she noted that "ornate structures, built after the plan of elaborate houses of many rooms, are not in good taste. . . ."[26]

WOMEN GARDEN WRITERS
The founding of the Garden Club of America in 1913 provided a national forum for amateurs like Anna Gilman Hill, who wrote the "Gardener's Miscellany" for the club's *Bulletin*, and Mrs. Francis King. King's first book, *The Well-Considered Garden* (1915), was followed by many others in multiple editions. Helena Rutherfurd Ely and Mabel Osgood Wright, both early members, already had several popular gardening books to their credit. The club was exclusive, favoring as members those from established families, and enjoyed, as the club's historian described it, the "atmosphere of a Colonial or pioneering past lingering about the gardens of the present."[27]

A garden tea party, Fort Wayne, Indiana. Photograph, c. 1900. Chicago Historical Society
Informal meals were often taken in gardens; this one is enlivened with rows of old-fashioned single hollyhocks clambering over the lattice fence.

Louise Beebe Wilder was equally sympathetic toward old gardens. As she revealed in her first book, *My Garden* (1916), "no pleasanter picture for our emulation can be called to mind than those little walled gardens of long ago—the trim straight paths, the little beds and narrow, straight borders. . . . " She was adamant in preferring perennials, commenting on annuals that "They give the garden a fugitive, unstable quality, like that felt in cities when everyone lives in an apartment and moves at least once a year, and there are no old families, or traditions, nor anything comfortably familiar and just as it always has been."[28]

Wilder's nine books and numerous articles for *Garden Magazine* and *House and Garden* were aimed at the home gardener, based on her own experience as a knowledgeable plantswoman. With her husband, architect Walter Robb Wilder, she had created a garden at their summer home "Balderbrae" near Suffern, New York, that was the subject of *My Garden* and *Colour in My Garden* (1918). It included a garden house, rustic pergolas, and as she recommended, trellises "painted white or very light green" and board edgings for the beds, "quaint and useful for unpretentious gardens."[29]

The Wilders separated about 1919 and Louise Wilder began a new garden,

"Little Balderbrae" in Bronxville, New York, which she described in *Adventures in My Garden and Rock Garden* (1924), *Adventures in a Suburban Garden* (1931), and *What Happens in My Garden* (1934). This garden included a stone pergola, and numerous stone walls for rock gardening, her abiding passion.

ARTISTS' GARDENS Many American artists joined their commuting contemporaries in the suburbs.[30] In 1912, painters Philip Leslie Hale and his wife, Lilian Westcott Hale, moved into a 1727 house in Dedham, Massachusetts, within easy reach of Boston. At "Sandy Down" their home grounds provided a refuge from an industrial present that was excluded from their paintings as well.

Lilian Hale's sensitive studies of languid figures in antiques-filled interiors portrayed an idealized and aestheticized New England domestic life. A description of her garden emphasized its similar enclosure and exclusion of disturbing elements. "There are old trees, untrimmed bushes, tall scraggy plants concealing paths that wind and twist. There is an old god-terminus in one shaded nook; there's a sun dial marking the 'happy hours,' and all around the hallowed spot, an old, old chain, festooned with lavender wisteria and pink roses, shuts in the glory of the garden, and shuts out only that which is less beautiful. No wonder that the canvases which come from her [Hale's] studio are calm, restrained, breathe loveliness, and carry peace."[31]

For many American artists, as for supporters of the Arts and Crafts movement, a beautiful home and garden were moral as well as aesthetic necessities. A writer in the *Artsman*, the official journal of the cooperative Rose Valley crafts community near Philadelphia, exclaimed unequivocally, "Inartistic homes ruin our manners and morals and wreck our nervous systems."[32]

Illustrator Alice Barber Stephens and her husband, Charles Stephens, an instructor at the Pennsylvania Academy, in 1905 bought an old stone barn in the Rose Valley community. The barn was converted into studios, and an irregular, open-plan house of stone and stucco was added on to it. A stream crossed by a stone bridge bordered the grounds, which included an old springhouse. An imposing pergola was the only structure added to the garden in keeping with the "simple and direct character" intended by resident architect William L. Price for the community.[33] For Alice Stephens, the move to the suburbs from Philadelphia was a positive one. "I can speak heartily of gain in strength in our new home with its touch of outdoor life. There is some loss of city life, but the gain more than balances it."[34]

Daniel Garber, a second-generation Impressionist, settled near Lumberville,

Lilian Westcott Hale
(1881–1963). AN OLD CHERRY
TREE. 1930. Oil on canvas,
30 x 25 in. The National
Academy Museum, New York
*Hale's garden in Dedham,
Massachusetts, was the setting
for the tall picket fence and gate.*

Pennsylvania, where he bought a complex of buildings including an old house, mill, and barn. His barn studio became the center of life at "Cuttalossa," and its north window, overlooking the flower garden, the setting for many paintings. As did other artist-gardeners, Garber saw his home and garden as aesthetic creations equivalent to his paintings. As he explained to a cousin in 1929: "To know me now you would have to know the place. Everyone knows it's half of me."[35]

    The artist colony in Cornish, New Hampshire, dated to the residence of sculp-

Joseph Sharp's studio, Taos, New Mexico. Postcard, c. 1920. Couse Family Archive

tor Augustus Saint-Gaudens in the 1880s. He was soon joined by painters Thomas Wilmer Dewing and his wife, Maria Oakey Dewing, who pioneered in gardening there. Dewing's design for his garden gates, a fretwork tracery of radiating spokes, appeared in simplified form in other gardens, including that of Saint-Gaudens.

By 1900, the Cornish gardening mania had encouraged the landscape talents of two residents, Charles Adams Platt and Rose Standish Nichols, and would shortly develop those of a third, Ellen Biddle Shipman. Frances Duncan, who wrote of the many significant Cornish gardens in *Century Magazine*, singled out the garden made by painter and etcher Stephen Parrish as the most satisfying as well as the most individual. She admired the pergola and vine-covered walls that enclosed the outdoor living area adjoining the old-fashioned flower beds, and took note of the outbuildings. "There is an ingenious disposal of the 'offices'—a studio and a workshop, a charming little toolhouse and a greenhouse. Instead of being objects which must skulk behind shrubbery, these . . . are yet made a part of the scheme."[36]

Entry gate, studio of Irving Couse, Taos, New Mexico. Postcard, c. 1920. Couse Family Archive
Adobe architecture and native stone were combined with traditional ornaments such as the birdbath in the garden of Irving and Virginia Couse.

The spectacular landscape of New Mexico attracted scores of painters at the turn of the century. Figure painter Irving Couse and his wife, Virginia, came to Taos in 1902 and in 1909 bought an old adobe house on a hillside with a ravishing view of the mountains. Here Virginia Couse laid out a garden in terraces planted with old-fashioned flowers watered from a nearby *acequia*, an irrigation ditch the farmers depended on.

As well as stone walls, the garden included stone seats and, in the entrance court, a stone birdbath. The garden became a destination for visitors and a model for others in

Pergola. "Rose Valley Farm,"
Moylan, Pennsylvania.
Photograph in Phebe Westcott
Humphreys, *The Practical
Book of Garden Architecture*
(*1914*)
*The Doric columns of the pergola
built by Charles and Alice
Barber Stephens were made of
concrete.*

Taos, including that of the Couses' neighbor, fellow artist J. H. Sharp. As one visitor described it, "There were pansies, sweet clove pinks, stalks of delphinium almost as tall as hollyhocks, lovely asters and dahlias, roses and chrysanthemums. Open spaces of green grass, too, and seats of rocks and paths leading to all sorts of unexpected little nooks."[37]

Artists from the San Francisco Bay Area settled in Carmel-by-the-Sea beginning in the 1890s. Gardens around the simple bungalows were minimal—the magnificent coastal scenery was the attraction. Noteworthy in one garden was the treehouse used as a study by writer Mary Austin, who enjoyed dressing as a native American.[38]

From now on it will be the little gardens—the home gardens planned, developed, and cared for by their owners—that determine the future of gardening in America.

F. F. ROCKWELL, *"An Era Ends,"* THE HOME GARDEN, 1950

Bauhaus *and the* Home Garden, 1930–1960

E UROPEAN MODERNISM IN ART HAD ARRIVED with great fanfare at the New York Armory Show of 1913. In 1929 the exhibition of International Style architecture at the Museum of Modern Art in New York introduced the public to the new aesthetic of abstract forms and industrial materials in building. The arrival in America of the leading Bauhaus designers fleeing Nazi Germany, and their welcome in the academic establishment—Walter Gropius and Marcel Breuer at Harvard University, Joseph Albers at Yale—meant the direct dissemination of their ideas to a new generation of architects.

In these decades when everything seemed to be coming apart economically, socially, and politically (the Great Depression, World War II, the Korean War, the Cold War, and the McCarthy menace), there was comfort to be had in the certainties of science and technology. For modernist architects, the house was a "machine for living," with function and technology rather than convention or style determining layout and materials. The new house Gropius designed for himself in 1937 in Lincoln, Massachusetts, for example, was a simple rectangle built of poured concrete slabs and steel with prefabricated plate-glass windows.

The new materials were seen to be both democratic and appropriate for any locale, precluding any vernacular elements that would suggest the past. As one architect wrote about their use in his own house and garden, "metal, asbestos cement board, glass and concrete are all the result of modern technology and by their very precise fabricated nature look well together. Unlike New England clapboard, or Southwestern adobe, they are appropriate to any region."[1] The past was to be abandoned in landscape design as in

Garden house, "Green Plains," Mathews, Virginia. Photograph, 1951. Collection F. H. Cabot
The circular brick garden house within the scalloped wall balanced a duck house of the same shape on the other side of the wall.

architecture. A 1955 graduate in landscape studies at the University of California, Berkeley, recalled that "we were told, primarily by our architectural professors, that the past was not only dead but useless in our quest for modernist beauty... clean, asymmetric, uncomplicated, democratic and socially expressive...."[2]

In the garden, this emphasis on function meant simplified layouts with convenience and easy care foremost. Characteristics of modernist buildings—factory-made materials with no applied ornament and flowing spaces lacking definite boundaries—began to appear in garden structures and layouts. California was in the forefront of this new garden design; the openness of house plans made possible by the California climate and the informality of life there encouraged gardens centered on swimming pools, patios, and terraces.

In the postwar years, amateur gardeners could not but be affected by the work of modernist landscape designers like Thomas Church, Garrett Eckbo, James Rose, and Dan Kiley. Gardens reflecting their use of asymmetrical layouts, arcs, diagonals, and abstract shapes were prominently featured in shelter magazines and how-to books. At the same time, the negation of the past demanded by a pure modernist aesthetic based on function rather than style paradoxically imbued the past with the allure of the forbidden. The modernist claim to have eliminated conventions of taste in favor of purity of design seems to have released a flood of ornamentation, of questionable taste at best, in American gardens. The ultimate failure of modernism to capture the imagination of the American home gardener was foreshadowed in Walter Gropius's own garden. Gropius's wife, Ise, claimed to know ninety birds personally and ornamented the grounds of their home with scores of traditional birdhouses and birdbaths.

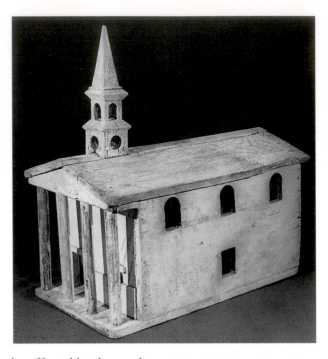

Church birdhouse, Kentucky. 1930s. Whitewashed wood, 27 x 25½ x 15 in. Private collection.

THE MODERNIST GARDEN

To update old homes, the authors of a book on revitalizing gardens, *New Gardens for Old* (1934), recommended formal gardens with box-bordered beds and a summerhouse or arbor as a focal point, but cautioned, "The indiscriminate use of pergolas, rose arbors, and much of the cheap ready-made latticework so often seen is to be deprecated...." That modernism had begun to affect popular garden design is evident even here. An enclosed outdoor living room bordered by shrubs and flowers, rather than a formal garden, was the preference of the authors and they noted a new taste for bright colors and simple shapes. "Beds divided into geometric patterns by low hedges and planted with a single color or two-tone effect seem to be coming into vogue. . . . Terraces paved with tile in gay solid colors are becoming popular."[3]

Henry B. Aul, garden columnist for the *New York Herald Tribune,* in his book *How to Plant Your Home Ground* (1953) pointed out "the ease with which the ranch house or other modern-type house built close to the grade can be related to the site." In the garden of such a contemporary house, he expected to find "a spacious paved lounge with convenient outdoor cooking facilities, a collection of ornamental trees, shrubs and smaller flowering plants and a well-built lawn along with . . . such architectural features as fences, gates, pools and shelters appropriate to the plan."[4] In an earlier book, *How to Build Garden Structures* (1950), Aul gave instructions for fences, pavings, grills, and tool houses using prefabricated materials.

Joseph E. Howland, an associate editor of *Better Homes and Gardens* and garden editor for *House Beautiful,* summed up the new garden aesthetic in *The House Beautiful Book of Gardens and Outdoor Living* (1958). For Howland, the focus of the garden was the patio or terrace, which "has grown from a back-yard picnic spot to the glamorous room you show off first to your guests. It fits so naturally today's informal way of living that it has become the most livable, most used room in the house."[5] In the gardens shown, free-form paving of concrete, flagstone, brick, or crushed stone occupied most of the space, with the lawn limited to small areas defined by mowing strips. As Howland put it, "We demand a floor for the garden equal in serviceability to the floor indoors. Often it is made of the same material."[6]

Plants and garden structures played minor roles. Evergreens, spring bulbs, and ornamental trees were featured, with ease of maintenance and year-round interest foremost. Low, curving walls or planting boxes rather than hedges defined garden spaces enclosed with louver fences. Howland recommended cinder blocks or chimney flue liners as planters and prefabricated structures as toolsheds. To provide shade for the paved areas, he suggested slat canopies supported by structural steel and touted the use of new materials like corrugated asbestos board rather than wood.

THE BARBECUE   Simple, easy-care gardens for outdoor living were in keeping with the increasing informality of suburban life centered on the nuclear family. The focus of many suburban patios was the outdoor grill, either freestanding or built into the patio wall. Various grills or fireboxes were readily available and many articles were written on their construction and use.[7]

Corinne Miller, in Tonganoxie, Kansas, collected stones, including geodes and arrowheads, for her impressive garden barbecue built in the 1930s. Offered either a honeymoon or a garden on her marriage, she chose the garden and formed an outstanding collection of irises laid out around a fish pond. The barbecue, however, was not only the focus of the Miller family's outdoor entertaining, but the centerpiece for the marriages of the Millers' daughter and granddaughter. For the ceremonies, the structure was covered with a trellis and decked with flowers.[8]

Owners of traditional homes often built a barbecue and chose a modernist layout for their grounds. Mr. and Mrs. Wolfgang Fyler, for example, did not change the old farmhouse that was their weekend home in Kitchawan, New York, but built a flagstone terrace with a grand outdoor fireplace next to the pond. Another flagstone terrace outside the kitchen door held rustic chairs and a dining table while a shed-roof studio with a wall of plate glass windows overlooked the garden.[9]

Barbecue in the garden of Corinne Miller, Tonganoxie, Kansas. Photograph by Kay Craine Martin. Courtesy Mrs. Gordon B. Hurlbut

THE GLAMOUR OF THE PAST

Modernist garden design struck many gardeners as cold, austere, and inimical both to a luxuriance of plants and any feeling for the past. A seductive alternative was offered by the garden restorations at Colonial Williamsburg, Virginia, begun in the 1930s. The Colonial Revival gardens created there were often photographed. Arthur A. Shurcliff, the landscape architect in charge, advised on many other garden restorations North and South, and these in turn were widely published. Interest in America's garden heritage had not waned, merely become less vocal.

Gardens begun in the 1930s and 1940s often combined modern paved terraces and patios with traditional axial layouts, pergolas, and geometric flower beds as did the garden of Mr. and Mrs. J. Dudley Clark in Wilmington, Delaware. Both the enclosing wall and the columns of their pergola were of poured concrete, however, rather than the traditional wood or stone.[10]

Many who had family properties with significant gardens, as did Dr. George

Carson house, Almaden, California. Photograph by Robert W. Kerrigan, 1936. Library of Congress, Historic American Buildings Survey, Washington, D.C.

Mr. and Mrs. J. E. Healy, who used this traditional adobe house as a weekend retreat, made an old-fashioned dooryard garden of raised beds, with a trellis for climbers.

Shattuck and his brother Henry, cherished and maintained them. The garden in Brookline, Massachusetts, that the Shattucks inherited in 1931 had belonged to Colonel Thomas Handasyd Perkins in the late eighteenth century. Nineteenth-century descendants had added a pergola and summerhouse along with hedges, a box garden, and a rock garden.[11]

Even in California, modernist gardens were not universally popular. Mr. and Mrs. J. E. Healy of Oakland bought the historic Carson adobe in Almaden, Santa Clara County, as a weekend retreat. Built as a modest three-room house in the 1840s, by 1930 its expanded L-shape invited a traditional dooryard garden. In the enclosed space the Healys formed raised beds edged with tile and brick and planted a mix of cacti, succulents, and hardy natives. A trellis against one wall held climbing roses. The old wooden barn, with its gable end dovecote, was also covered in climbers.[12]

The most upmarket of the shelter magazines, the venerable *House and Garden* under the direction of Richardson Wright, often featured both old houses and axial plan gardens as well as garden structures looking back to the past. The readership of the mag-

azine included those who felt no need to demonstrate either the moral earnestness or modishness implied by modernist design. They would have read with interest an article on "Wye Plantation" in Maryland, recently restored by Arthur Shurcliff, and given two octagonal garden houses with bell roofs and fretwork railings. Of equal interest would have been a hexagonal summerhouse with a pagoda roof in the "Baroque Garden" photographed for the March 1947 issue. An article on "Fences with a Purpose" the next year recommended traditional pickets, colonial fretwork, and Thomas Jefferson's serpentine brick wall, as well as fences of woven redwood strips and louvers.[13]

The magazine's *Book of Gardens* (1955) included only two photographs of barbecues but numerous ones of white picket fences, arbors, rustic pergolas, and summerhouses. The toolshed shown was a neoclassical cube with a dovecote under the pyramidal roof. The one major concession to modern life, given a whole chapter, was the swimming pool and its surrounding terrace designed for outdoor entertaining.

More down-home publications also advised on traditional garden structures. In

John Falter (1910–1982). BILL's BIRD HOUSE. 1948. Tempera on board, 19¾ x 18½ in. American Illustrators Gallery, New York
This illustration of a small town shop selling whirligigs and birdhouses appeared on the cover of the Saturday Evening Post.

a series of articles for *The Home Garden,* Henry B. Aul drew suggestions for pergolas, arches, arbors, and garden seats, disagreeing with "garden designers of the modern school who belittle the type of formal design that employs a bench as a symmetrically placed terminal feature."[14] In the same series, an article on "Gates and Entrances" by another writer provided drawings for traditional picket fences and Chinese fretwork gates.[15]

"GREEN PLAINS" When Mr. and Mrs. F. Higginson Cabot went house hunting in Tidewater, Virginia, in 1937, they sought, as Currie Cabot wrote, "old woodwork, and boxwood in a garden, farm land, the river. . . ." At "Green Plains" in Mathews County they found a 1798 brick house and a scalloped brick garden wall that together with the "overarching box trees" gave an "almost tangible" feeling of the past. Currie Cabot began the restoration of the garden, envisioning one that combined "the beauties of every old Virginia house and garden we had seen with the Governor's Palace at Williamsburg thrown in for good measure."[16]

The outbuildings were central to "Green Plains," as they were to all early working farms or plantations, and they featured prominently in the restoration of the garden. The entrance drive was moved to approach from the side rather than between the scalloped garden wall and the line of outbuildings. The original office and square smokehouse were complemented with a circular duck house designed by Edward J. Mathews, Currie Cabot's brother, who advised on the restoration of the house. A balancing circular garden house within the scalloped wall functioned as a toolshed.

J. Horace McFarland in his
garden at "Breeze Hill."
Photograph, 1942. Smithson-
ian Institution, Archives of
American Gardens, Washing-
ton, D.C. Garden Club of
America Collection
*Noted rosarian J. Horace
McFarland is seen here in the
front garden of his home in
Harrisburg, Pennsylvania, with
the gazebo dating to the 1870s.*

WINDMILLS AND WHIRLIGIGS   The freedom from
convention fostered by modernism encouraged imaginative and uninhibited home gardeners across the country to incorporate all sorts of manufactured objects in their gardens — plastic flamingos, laden donkeys doubling as planters, and lawn-grazing deer
could all be found there. Equally popular were homemade whirligigs, diminutive lighthouses, and windmills. Whole towns occasionally got into the act.

The small town of Neosho, Missouri, became known for its flower boxes. Wheelbarrows, wooden barrels, abandoned woodstoves and washing machines, even baby carriages were appropriated as planters and filled with marigolds, salvia, morning glories,
and bulbs in spring. A visitor noted that "Upstairs offices boast boxes on windowsills.
Scarlet geraniums fill baskets suspended from street-light poles. Even trash receptacles
are topped with petunias."[17]

A directory of 1960 described home gardens across the country boasting such decorations. The Huettner family garden in Lakota, Iowa, begun in 1933, was enclosed with a white picket fence and had a lily pool, rock garden, and miniature windmill. Mr. and Mrs. Fred K. Smith of Omaha, Nebraska, included in their city garden a wagon wheel painted white, a diminutive gnome holding a lantern, and an ornamental duck. The garden in Pine Hill, South Dakota, of Mrs. Ernest Rhodes was home to a pair of wrought-iron peacocks.[18]

Dr. Thomas Sinclair's garden in Houston, Texas, was entered through an arched arbor and backed with two enormous white-painted trellises for climbers. The central feature was a rectangular pool surrounded by iris and overlooked by a miniature mill complete with clapboard siding and topped by a cupola.[19]

A painter who began a garden on Long Island in the 1950s was equally uninhibited, although the results proved to be much more elegant. The most salient feature of Gerson Leiber's garden is the structure provided by its many elegant trellises and enframing hedges of privet, with box, yew, and other evergreens. When he began the garden he confessed that, "No one I knew was doing anything like this . . . there was no plan. I just did a bit here, then something over in another direction. It was like starting a painting—you just work at it until something starts to come out."[20]

Stately, blue-painted trellises, pierced by arched doorways and surmounted by finials and gables, form screen walls that enclose formal parterres of brick paths and box-edged beds. A grape arbor of weathered posts and crossbeams used for outdoor dining is echoed by a wisteria arbor, the entrance to another garden enclosure. The beds in the vegetable and cutting garden are divided by brick paths and backed by a picket fence. One of the garden structures there is the familiar neoclassical cube topped with a pyramidal roof next to a taller one with board-and-batten siding.

J. HORACE MCFARLAND
Home gardeners often specialized in plants that suggested appropriate structures. Iris collections, for example, needed pools to be seen to best advantage. Roses were often given separate enclosures and

Rustic summerhouse at "Breeze Hill." Photograph by J. Horace McFarland. Smithsonian Institution, Archives of American Gardens, Washington, D.C. Garden Club of America Collection

This rustic structure stood at one end of the axial path through the garden where four beds were centered on a sundial. Another garden enclosure held more than 300 varieties of roses.

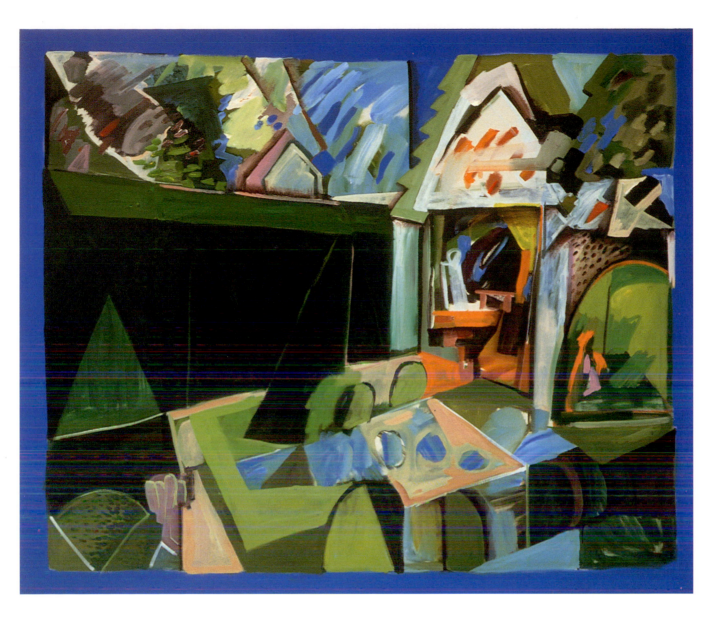

Gerson Leiber (b. 1921). WHITE TRELLIS. 1996. Oil on canvas, 22 x 26 in. Collection the artist

Gerson Leiber began his garden at East Hampton, Long Island, in the 1950s, incorporating such traditional structures as trellises, arbors, and garden houses within hedged enclosures. His recent series of garden paintings suggests the richness of both structure and planting there.

climbing varieties demanded trellises and arbors. The American Rose Society included among its members Thomas Johnson of Lake Odessa, Michigan, who began his garden in 1910—by 1960 the garden included 850 feet of trellis and more than 1,200 plants. A. E. Albera of Denver, Colorado, specialized in hybrid teas that he grew in full sun but sheltered under redwood slats supported on cast-iron pillars. W. C. Williamson's garden in Tulsa, Oklahoma, surrounded an outdoor terrace and featured a fourteen-foot-high hybrid tea climber on a white-painted arbor.[21]

A noted photographer of estate gardens and a printer of horticultural books and seed catalogues, J. Horace McFarland began to garden seriously in middle age when he bought a Victorian house on two acres outside Philadelphia in 1909. He described making the garden at "Breeze Hill" in *My Growing Garden* (1915). Disgusted with gardens he had seen—as he put it "the very sight of some gardens was irritating, because of their expensive elaboration"—he determined to seek the "real garden knowledge which is found only with the spade and the rake, and amongst the seeds and plants, and bulbs and roots and vines of American hardiness."[22]

He intended his garden not only to be "home-like" but to reflect his home state in featuring native plants. As he wrote, "the old features have been zealously preserved, and the new plantings and placings adopted to them. The result is a mature and *home-ly* (please note the hyphen and what it means) beauty that could not have been had in a generation if we had 'started afresh.'"[23] Thus he retained the Victorian pergola on the front lawn and designed a rustic one for the new garden. This garden, on an axis from the living room of the house, had four rectangular flower beds centered on a sundial and backed by a hedge.

McFarland developed a passion for climbing roses; "Breeze Hill" was to shelter more than three hundred varieties in the 1940s. To support his collection, McFarland contrived, with native ingenuity, eight-foot posts of gas pipe linked with arches of strap iron, and noted happily, "There are of course many other ways to do this, some of them more expensive, but I have not seen any that gave a pleasanter effect."[24]

A GARDEN COTTAGE Gardens and their structures were not only sources of great pleasure to their makers, they could also quite literally provide a refuge. In 1881, Brooklyn merchant and recent widower Charles Foster purchased a Gothic Revival house in Morristown, New Jersey, as a permanent residence for himself and his four-year-old daughter, Caroline. "Fosterfields" was a working farm which Charles Foster ran efficiently; as his daughter grew up, he encouraged her active partic-

ipation. Caroline also played an important role in the social life of Morristown, which by the 1890s had become a millionaires' suburb, and enjoyed as well shooting, fishing, and carpentry.

Caroline's skill with the hammer and saw was put to good use when she determined to build a cottage as a refuge from her increasingly irascible father, and as a place to entertain friends. She modeled the cottage on the one-room colonial kitchen, an icon of the Colonial Revival, and on houses seen on summers on Cape Cod. She constructed it herself using chestnut trees from the property, and secondhand lumber, window sashes, and floorboards. The massive fireplace was assembled from stones she had gathered in the woods. On its completion in 1919, Caroline proudly recorded that the total spent on the "Temple of Abiding Peace" was only two hundred dollars.[25]

The cottage was given a coat of white paint and green shutters and for the next four decades was the focus of Caroline Foster's gardening as well as entertaining. Her garden, arranged in irregular beds of densely planted old-fashioned perennials, was entered through a picket gate in a stone wall. Two rustic trellises supported roses. After her father's death in 1927, Caroline ran the farm and worked in her garden, dressed as she always had in a skirt with a man's shirt, jacket, tie, and straw hat, until well into her eighties, when failing eyesight limited her activities.[26]

In times of great uncertainty, we search more diligently for stability.
The past will not change; it is comforting and at rest. It offers great security.
What better place to gain this sense than in a home we perceive as timeless,
and in tune with the values of earlier and more straightforward times?

McKie W. Roth, Jr. *"Why Build an Early American House?,"* Early American Life, 1985

LOOKING BACK — THE RECENT PAST

THE UNITED STATES, A CONFIDENT SUPERPOWER at the beginning of the 1960s, by the next decade had undergone a series of economic and political shocks, the assassination of President John F. Kennedy in 1963 perhaps the most poignant. Reaction focused on the Vietnam War. The last American ground troops left Vietnam in 1973, the same year that the oil embargo demonstrated how dependent America was on the global economy. Recession, inflation, obsolete factories and stagnant wages, growing extremes of wealth and poverty, urban riots, and the free-floating anxiety that seemed characteristic of the atomic age created a compelling sense of things out of joint.

With the approach of the bicentennial, the country's attention turned once again to America's past with both nostalgia and relief. As the historic preservation movement gained new vigor, old farmhouses again became desirable as weekend or summer homes. Even the excesses of Victorian architecture and gardens began to be viewed with affection. Just as had happened in the 1870s, the renewed interest in old houses and gardens that surfaced in the 1970s was reflected in popular magazines and new specialized ones, like *Early American Life,* started in 1969, and *Colonial Homes,* begun in 1975.

The 1970s saw the beginnings of postmodernism in architecture and the reintroduction of ornament with whimsical and self-conscious references to traditional styles. New suburban developments began to play on the fantasy of America's rural past, offering farmhouse and barn look-alikes rather than split-levels with attached garages. Magazines like *Country Home* and *Country Journal* presented a spruced-up and sanitized version of life "down home." Even *The Old House Journal*, begun as an informative newsletter for restorers of older homes, became a glossy magazine in 1986 and featured

Edward Giobbi (b. 1926). JACOB WRESTLING WITH THE ANGEL. 1991.
Charcoal, distemper, and oil on paper laminated to linen, 75 x 44½ in. Private collection
*The pergola overlooking the pond in painter Ed Giobbi's garden in Katonah, New York,
dates to the beginning of the century and often appears in the background of his paintings.*

articles on garden layouts and old-fashioned plants appropriate for eighteenth- and nineteenth-century homes.

The explosion of technology in the 1980s and 1990s, resulting in instant fortunes and creating ever more ephemeral celebrities, has fueled a growing hunger for the hand-made, the authentic, and the permanent. We dream of a time when life was real rather than virtual, when the actual process of daily living was both physically demanding and sensually rewarding. As a nation, we have taken up gardening as a panacea and we furnish our gardens with those things that remind us of a more human and humane past.

EVERYTHING OLD IS NEW AGAIN
Old-fashioned garden structures as well as heirloom plants are now gratefully embraced by everyone from landscape professionals to backyard gardeners. Connecticut garden designer Nancy McCabe constructs rustic arbors, fences, gates, and seats for her own garden and for those of clients. A whimsical Chinese pagoda birdhouse reminiscent of eighteenth-century follies is a focal point of her garden; she has designed an equally charming Gothic Revival doghouse for a friend. Decorator Bunny Williams, a neighbor, has a rustic arbor of natural locust posts in her vegetable garden; its mixture of flowers and herbs, brick paths, and rectangular beds recalls colonial ones. Seeds for old-fashioned flowers come from Monticello's Center for Historic Plants, only one of a number of sources for heirloom varieties.

Hitch Lyman. Greek Revival folly designed for his garden in Trumansburg, New York. 1992. Photograph by D. DeCesare
Hitch Lyman's Doric temple, incorporating four rescued porch columns, faces his Greek Revival house across a pond and meadow.

The temple summerhouse has reappeared in gardens. In Lansing, Michigan, builder Robert J. Morris designed a miniature Ionic temple to enclose a garden hot tub. It was so successful that he formed a company to manufacture prefabricated garden houses in traditional architectural styles ranging from Greek Revival to Gothic. On a grander scale, a New York City couple have transformed their weekend home, a 1790s farmhouse in southeastern Connecticut, into a Palladian villa with an Ionic entry portico. A rotunda serves as the gateway into a garden laid out in geometric beds bordered in box.[1]

Traditional summerhouses, trellises, and pergolas, if not rotundas, are available ready-made across the country and turn up in backyards as well as in formal gardens. Other home gardeners prefer to build their own. In Hillsborough, North Carolina, Karen and David Wysocki came upon a pamphlet, "Beautifying the Home Grounds," published in 1926 by the Southern Forest Products Association. Inspired by the drawings and

Summerhouse designed and built by Karen and David Wysocki, Hillsborough, North Carolina. Photograph by Kent Murray, c. 1980
The Wysocki's latticed pergola, suggested by a 1926 pattern book, is reminiscent of many turn-of-the-century summer-houses.

photographs of pergolas, the Wysockis built one of their own design to enclose their back-yard patio, doing all the work themselves. The Wysockis were so enthusiastic about the results that they reprinted the pamphlet in the belief that "gardens and garden structures are possible for ordinary folks who can't afford large estates or full-time yard workers. The pleasures of outdoor living are for everyone, and the ideas for creating your special spaces are right here!"[2]

Dennis Broderick's garden in Merriam, Kansas, began modestly with a small pond, expanded to more ponds linked by waterfalls and embellished with a fountain, and culminated recently with a custom-built octagonal summerhouse perched on a deck. With the exception of its eighteenth-century bell roof, the structure recalls Mark Twain's octagonal study.[3]

WALLS AND FENCES Walled gardens turn up everywhere. Designer Peter Wooster put up a picket fence around a sizable chunk of his side yard in Connecticut and made a riotious flower garden in geometric beds centered on a shelter-ing wooden parasol, an idea dating to the early nineteenth century. Painter Raymond Han's kitchen garden, on a farm near Cooperstown, New York, is delimited by a white fence with Chippendale fretwork panels. Choisy Blank's rose garden in California's Napa

Valley is also fence-enclosed, and entered through an arched trellis covered with roses, reminiscent of those popular one hundred years ago.[4]

Dr. Dale Gordon Gutman and his wife, Ann Knight Gutman, avid collectors of American antiques, have housed them in "Scottwood," an eighteenth-century brick house in Kentucky. The Gutmans are equally enthusiastic gardeners. Just as they have decorated their home with murals recalling nineteenth-century works by Rufus Porter, they have enclosed their garden with a white picket fence and furnished it with an appealing toolshed, indebted in its proportions and steeply pitched pyramidal roof to early-nineteenth-century prototypes.[5]

The design of Judith Janke's kitchen garden in Charlottesville, Virginia, was suggested by the one at "Ash Lawn," President James Monroe's modest circa 1800 estate nearby. Enclosed in a picket fence, the forty-foot-square garden of raised, wood-bordered beds is backed with a garden shed that echoes the classic southern "dog-trot" cabin of two rooms separated by a covered breezeway.[6]

Lois Dodd (b. 1927). LAUNDRY LINE, RED, WHITE, BLACK AND PITCHFORK. 1979. Oil on linen, 36 x 54 in. Collection the artist
Painter Lois Dodd has made an old privy into a focal point of her garden in Cushing, Maine; in summer, it serves as a trellis for vines.

OPPOSITE: Joellyn Duesberry (b. 1945). GATE TO THE GARDEN. 1997. Oil on linen, 30 x 22 in. Collection Dr. and Mrs. Gary Van der Ark
Landscape painter Joellyn Duesberry's perennial garden in Littleton, Colorado, incorporates Conestoga wagon wheels and an old horse-drawn plow as well as modern iron gates and trellises.

In southwest Ohio, Dr. Richard B. Studebaker and his wife, Sue, bought a late-eighteenth-century farmhouse and furnished it with a notable collection of American antiques, including many textiles, Sue Studebaker's special interest. The formal garden of boxwood-bordered beds centered on a sundial is enclosed with a white picket fence. The central path terminates in a dovecote, an inventive variant on the neoclassical cube.[7] The pool house is modeled on the bell-roofed pavilions at "Mount Vernon," as are many other garden houses across the country.

OLD GARDENS EMBELLISHED Louise Beebe Wilder's beloved "Balderbrae," discussed earlier, was reluctantly abandoned in 1920; it has been rescued and brilliantly rejuvenated by designer David Easton and his partner. The original stone garden cottage served as the model for a large home with two porch wings. Remaining pergolas link the house, cottage, and gardens, enclosed in the original stone walls.

At "Glenstone," the Turner family's eighteenth-century property in northern Virginia, a formal boxwood garden was made in the 1920s by three Turner sisters. In the 1980s, the garden was expanded by Turner Reuter, the son of one of the sisters, and his wife, Nancy. A cutting garden, a box garden centered on a fountain, and a perennial garden were fitted within the old garden's boundaries formed of massive American box. A pyramidal lath roof with finial, reminiscent of those on nineteenth-century lath summerhouses, was placed at the midpoint of the pergola dividing the cutting garden from the perennial garden. In the cutting garden, a hexagonal structure with a pointed roof recalling eighteenth-century ones, was intended for tool storage. A whimsical elevated perch, much like that of painter William Morris Hunt's a century earlier, was strategically placed to give a view of the entire garden.[8]

Craufurd and Nancy Goodwin bought a Georgian Revival house in Hillsborough, North Carolina, in 1977. The original "Montrose" had been built in 1842, and outbuildings, including a smokehouse with attached privy, remained. Nancy Goodwin's garden, run as a nursery until 1994, occupies the space that was once the kitchen garden. The centerpiece is a lath trellis house that in silhouette echoes the nineteenth-century buildings outside the enclosing picket fence.[9]

Old outbuildings become the focus of other gardens. Floral designer Renny Reynolds on his Bucks County, Pennsylvania, farm, for example, has given a gingerbread hen house a wisteria-draped pergola and arranged beside it herb gardens bordered in dwarf box and centered on a sundial and an urn.[10]

Garden house of Dale and
Ann Gutman, Midway,
Kentucky. Photograph 1997
*The Gutmans' toolshed looks
back to neoclassical outbuildings.*

STARTING FROM SCRATCH
Colonial Williamsburg in Virginia, Old Sturbridge Village in Massachusetts, and similar restorations of early houses and gardens continue to influence new designs. A house in Raleigh, North Carolina, was modeled after the Solomon Richardson saltbox in Old Sturbridge Village and given an appropriate garden of herbs and flowers in plank-edged raised beds that occupies most of the backyard. In Cartersville, Georgia, a new home of old brick was inspired by "Holly Hill," an eighteenth-century Maryland house. The garden, of diamond-shaped beds outlined with box and bordered by brick pathways, is enclosed in a white picket fence.[11]

Having grown up surrounded by historic Pennsylvania stone houses, Earl Jamison built a similar house on forty acres of empty farmland in Bucks County. Now surrounded by appropriate outbuildings—springhouses, a garden house, a chicken house, and a fanciful gazebo with a dovecote in its peaked roof—the stone house looks as though it has always been there. Wooden fences in a delightful variety of forms, pierced with stone arches or wooden gates, define garden areas.

FOLK FURNITURE AND THE RUSTIC REVIVAL
The Adirondack chair made of flat boards was patented in 1903 and is still being manufactured today. Rustic twig furniture, handmade in quantity to fill the Great Camps of the Adirondacks and other north woods vacation spots, has proved equally durable. This is furniture that must be handmade as each piece depends on the particular eccentricities of the saplings and tree roots used in its construction. The respect now accorded folk art means that the twig furniture made by craftsmen such as Joe Little Creek in Georgia is too expensive for garden use, but widely published instructions must mean that a lot of us are making our own.[12]

Rustic structures like those in New York City's Central Park and elsewhere that were so influential beginning in the 1860s are popular again. Craftsmen such as David Robinson, who has made rustic structures for Central Park, cannot keep up with the

Garden house of Richard and Sue Studebaker, Dayton, Ohio
The Studebakers' neoclassical dovecote stands in a parterre garden of box-bordered beds centered on a sundial.

Left: Gazebo in the garden of Marvin Davis, Woodstock, New York. Photograph courtesy of Romancing the Woods, Inc., Woodstock, New York
This rustic gazebo made by carpenter Robert O'Leary for Marvin Davis's weekend home inspired "Romancing the Woods," a business reproducing nineteenth-century rustic structures and furniture.

James M. Steinmeyer. Plan of "Balderbrae," Pomona, New York. Gouache on paper, 8 x 10 in.
Designer David Easton's new house and restored garden, as well as the old garden house, nestle within the original walls of Louise Beebe Wilder's beloved "Balderbrae."

· BALDERBRAE ·

demand. The rustic gazebos at Mohonk Mountain House in New Paltz, New York, begun as a boardinghouse in 1870, inspired New Yorker Marvin Davis to commission a similar shelter for his Catskill retreat in Woodstock, New York. The appealing open gazebo, perched on the edge of a cliff with an expansive view of the mountains, was so successful that Davis decided to start a small business in partnership with wood craftsman Robert O'Leary to reproduce other rustic nineteenth-century garden furnishings. The Eastern red cedar that Andrew Jackson Downing had recommended in the nineteenth century was still available in abundance and there was a renewed demand for rustic work. "Romancing the Woods," as the business is called, took off and now offers benches, observation towers, bridges, fences, and gates as well as a variety of gazebos.[13] Many companies across the country now make such structures. Others, such as John Danzer, offer reproductions of more formal American garden furniture.

BIRDHOUSES AND GAZING GLOBES Birdhouses, both antique and new ones, in traditional styles that are available mass produced, have become ubiquitous in American gardens. Craftsmen across the country turn out one-of-a-kind examples that are snapped up as soon as they are made. A 1987 exhibition of architect-designed birdhouses organized by the Parrish Art Museum in Southampton, New York, that was followed by an astoundingly successful auction, began a trend of birdhouse fundraisers that continues unabated.

Gardeners welcome the vertical exclamation points given by birdhouses on poles, and use them as supports for the vines that are as popular now as they were at the turn of the century. Mary Schroer's garden in Urbana, Illinois, incorporates several, both as shelters for birds and as props for her collection of climbing honeysuckles. The architectural birdhouses have particular appeal for her, as for so many others. She writes, "I like the way two short pieces of dowel and a bit of leftover cornice transform a plain birdhouse into a temple, or how a spire on top creates a church."[14]

Whole garden areas are devoted to birdhouses. In the South, James Cramer and Dean Johnson have filled a succession of gardens with their collection of antique examples and appealing new ones crafted by Johnson. Sharon Abroms, who gardens in Atlanta, Georgia, has a birdhouse garden where she has gathered her collection into a community of buildings, among them a replica of "Tara" from *Gone with the Wind.* Penny Vogel, whose garden is in Estacata, Oregon, has incorporated a village of birdhouses crafted by her neighbor Millie Kiggins that includes an inn, a store, and a chicken coop.[15]

Landscape architect Loring Underwood's *The Garden and Its Accessories* (1907) had recommended a gazing globe on a pedestal as a garden centerpiece. These silvered glass spheres have been made for centuries, but they became popular in American gardens in the early 1900s. Together with sundials and birdbaths, gazing globes have again found a place in the garden, if no longer as the center of symmetrical beds.

Ken Moore of the North Carolina Botanical Garden at Chapel Hill became a gaz-

Sandra Shelton's bird feeder, Vienna, Missouri. Photograph courtesy of Marie's Hollow Herb Farm, Vienna, Missouri

ing globe addict after buying a large blue one, along with two painted concrete flamingos, on a trip to Florida. At first the globes rested conventionally on a concrete base until Moore realized how reflections enhanced the garden plantings and that the globes could be used as decorative structures in their own right. He placed a row of them on pedestals stretching across a meadow, put a few on the ground to reflect overhead foliage, and clustered others in the grass.[16]

BITS AND PIECES   Nineteenth-century garden furnishings, twig tables and chairs, cast-iron benches and urns, and any interesting architectural structures, are understandably popular and fetch surprisingly high prices. The desire to incorporate a bit of the American past in the home garden has created a demand even for the detritus of old houses and gardens—disembodied finials, unattached columns and trellises, random flower pots, and wooden plant stands. Antique dealers across the country have scoured attics and barns for these former discards and display them imaginatively in appealing small shops. For her own garden, shop owner Sandra Shelton of Vienna, Missouri, constructed a bird feeder out of a turned balustrade from her husband's family home and topped it with a finial; she also uses old trellises as decorative accents. Michael Trapp's West Cornwall, Connecticut, garden, tumbling precipitously down toward Mill Brook in rock-walled terraces, brilliantly incorporates American architectural fragments, most notably turned porch and stair balustrades, together with traditional garden ornaments.

The passion for garden decoration, an offshoot of postmodernism in architecture, has encouraged the use of objects previously unthinkable to conventional gardeners concerned with good taste. Felder Rushing, author of *Passalong Plants* (1993) and long an advocate of down-home ornaments for the garden such as tire planters, or bottle trees or even pink flamingos, is being joined by the mainstream. As columnist Margery Guest confessed in the *American Horticulturist,* "I once thought whirligigs were in the same class as those wooden figurines of bent-over people with big butts. But then I saw several in a friend's garden, twirling gracefully among the digitalis and achillea." An article in *Southern Living* recently advised home gardeners to "Explore flea markets and junk shops. . . . Shop yard sales and secondhand stores. . . . Rummage through salvage yards for ironwork and architectural fragments to display like statuary in a planting bed. Check your own garage or attic for a favorite personal memento, such as an ancient bicycle or wagon, to feature imaginatively as sculpture in your garden."[17]

PLYWOOD COWS

Pink flamingos, burros, miniature lighthouses, and windmills still turn up in home gardens, but they have been recently overtaken by herds of painted Holstein cattle and flocks of fuzzy plywood sheep, off-hand references to America's rural past. The two-dimensional cow even surfaces in urban California, where novelist and architectural critic Leon Whiteson has created a tamed jungle in the backyard of his Hollywood cottage, its center a redwood arch smothered in vines. His is a garden rich in associations. Certain plants recall his childhood in Zimbabwe, or years spent in Spain and Greece. The garden is studded with objects having personal significance, among them a totem pole crowned by an upended chandelier, a symbolic ruin constructed of brick, and a black-and-white plywood cow, the gift of a friend who had died of AIDS. The garden is also home to a burro planter holding a sago palm, a miniature train filled with petunias and violets, and several fountains fashioned out of halved whisky barrels and ready-made concrete statuary.[18]

LOOKING BACK

Gardens, no less than houses and clothing, undergo the vicissitudes of fashion. Even vernacular gardens and their structures

Tire planter and paling fence, Dean Riddle garden, Phoenicia, New York
Dean Riddle's garden with its rectangular, stone-bordered beds and fence of hardwood saplings suggests colonial gardens. His tire planter seems surprisingly at home.

often reflect current styles, if unselfconsciously. The landscape garden, originating in England, and in evidence here by 1800, swept away geometric beds of shrubs and flowers, and occasionally the flowers themselves. The garden structures remained and their practical functions also offered the opportunity for displays of status, erudition, whimsy, and ingenuity. Summerhouses gave cooling repose, even in the most utilitarian of gardens. In pleasure gardens they provided an occasion for classical temples, Chinese pagodas, or stately Palladian rotundas. Grape arbors functioned as green walls separating garden areas. A decorative virtue was made of necessary houses, as privies were termed then, and other functional outbuildings. Birdhouses were architecture in miniature.

In the nineteenth-century garden, structures ranged from severe neoclassical cubes and Greek temples to Gothic flights of architectural fancy. At midcentury, the picturesque garden, championed by Andrew Jackson Downing, demanded rustic gazebos and seats, if not mock ruins and Gothic follies. Successful farmers and craftsmen, as well as merchants and industrialists, could afford to build houses in the latest style, and to lay out their gardens in geometric beds of annuals or with picturesque pathways and shrubbery and often both. Birdhouses were ubiquitous and were made in all of the popular architectural styles.

By 1900, nostalgia for the colonial era had overtaken the country; arbors, trellises, fences, and garden houses modeled on eighteenth-century ones could be found everywhere. The Arts and Crafts movement encouraged out-of-door living and the use of piazzas, as porches were termed, and pergolas. Gardens were floriferous as a traditional perennial garden, which filled to bursting with old-fashioned flowers became popular again. Within decades, however, the impact of modernist landscape design on the home garden became evident in the use of paved patios, barbecues and swimming pools. Flower gardening reached a nadir in the 1950s with the emphasis on easy-care shrubs and trees. But modernism failed to sustain the imagination of the American home gardener. Its elimination of style and ornament in favor of pure function likewise eliminated the pleasure afforded by decorative structures and furnishings.

Americans, as de Tocqueville wrote in 1840, have always preferred the useful to the beautiful, but we seem also to have required that the useful be decorative and appeal to our distinctive and often quirky tastes. We are a nation of individuals but we have, since even before the Revolution, first identified ourselves as American. Our gardens, no matter how much they have evidenced borrowings from other countries and other times, have been American ones, often determinedly so, and no more so than at present.

Notes

Ornaments *and* Necessities *in* Colonial Gardens

1. Rev. Peter Whitney, *The History of the County of Worcester* (1793), 235.

2. Barbara Wells Sarudy, "A late eighteenth-century 'tour' of Baltimore gardens" (1989), 136.

3. See Barbara Wells Sarudy's fascinating account: "A Chesapeake Craftsman's Eighteenth-Century Gardens" (1989). William Faris's diary is in the collection of the Maryland Historical Society.

4. Alice B. Lockwood, ed., *Gardens of Colony and State* (1931), vol. 2: 80.

5. See Francis Higginson, "New Englands Plantation" (1929) and Helen Evertson Smith, "An Ancient Garden" (1906).

6. Rev. William Bentley, The, *Diary of William Bentley, D. D.* (reprint, 1962), vol. 1: 180.

7. Quoted in Bradford L. Rauschenberg, "An American Eighteenth-Century Garden Seat in the Chinese Taste" (1997), 5.

8. Ibid.

9. Quoted in Rita Susswein Gottesman, *The Arts and Crafts in New York 1726–1776* (1938), 113–14.

10. Robert Beverly, *The History and Present State of Virginia* (1947), 299.

11. The plans for these gardens, drawn by Moravian surveyor Philip Christina Gottlieb Reuter, are the earliest known in America with plants lists, most unusual in documenting utilitarian rather than ornamental gardens. See Flora Ann Bynum, *Old Salem Garden Guide* (1979), 56–62.

12. Elise Pinckney, ed., *The Letterbook of Eliza Lucas Pinckney 1739–1762* (1972), 6.

13. Lockwood, *Gardens of Colony and State,* vol. 2:145, 149.

14. Anne Grant, *Memoirs of an American Lady* (American ed., 1876), 236.

15. Quoted in Peter Martin, *The Pleasure Gardens of Virginia* (1991), 206.

16. See Florence M. Montgomery, *Printed Textiles* (1970), 144–46 and Catherine Lynn, *Wallpaper in America* (1980), 103–6.

17. R. B. Leuchars, "Notes on Gardens and Gardening in the Neighborhood of Boston" (1850), 59.

18. Bentley, *The Diary of William Bentley, D.D.* vol. 1: 264.

19. Letter of November 15, 1819, Pennsylvania Historical Society quoted in Lockwood, vol. 1: 344. See also Mary G. Kimball, "The Revival of the Colonial" (1927), 3.

20. James D. Kornwolf, "The Picturesque in the American Garden and Landscape before 1800," R. P. Maccubbin and Peter Martin, eds., *British and American Gardens in the Eighteenth Century* (1984), 98, and George C. Rogers, Jr., "Gardens and Landscapes in Eighteenth Century South Carolina" (1983), 151–52. A good introduction to these English gardens is Kimberly Rorschach, *The Early Georgian Landscape Garden* (1983).

21. Quoted in Kristin Burton, "The Garden of Colonial Flowers at Monroe Tavern" (1997), 51.

22. Peter Martin, *The Pleasure Gardens of Virginia*, 72, 77.

23. H. Chandlee Forman, *Old Buildings, Gardens and Furniture in Tidewater Maryland* (1967), 27.

24. Quoted in Sarudy, "A Chesapeake Craftsman's Eighteenth-Century Gardens," 147.

25. Michael T. Trostel, "The Maryland Orangeries" (1996) 3, 4, and Billie Sherrill Britz, "The Orangery in England and America" (1996), 598–99. See also May Woods and Arete Warren, *Glass Houses* (1988).

26. See Benjamin Smith, "Letters from William Hamilton to his Private Secretary" (1905), and Britz, "The Orangery," 598.

27. Lockwood, *Gardens of Colony and State*, vol. 1: 282.

28. Julia Margaret Conner diary (1827) quoted in Darrell Spencer, *The Gardens of Salem* (1997), 46.

29. Grant, *Memoirs of an American Lady*, 115, 111.

30. Richard M. Candee, "Strictly for the Birds" (1996), 13.

THE NEW REPUBLIC, 1780–1810

1. Merrill D. Peterson, ed., *The Portable Thomas Jefferson* (1977), 290.

2. Edward Augustus Kendall, *Travels through the Northern Parts of the United States 1807–1808,* 3 vols. (New York: Riley, 1809) and others. The term first appeared in print in the 1742 second edition of Stephen Switzer's *Iconographic Rustica* (London, 1718). As late as 1827 John Lowell described his estate "Bromley Vale" near Boston as a *ferme ornée*. See Tamara Platkins Thornton, *Cultivating Gentlemen* (1989), 111.

3. Frederick Doveton Nicholas and Ralph E. Griswold, *Thomas Jefferson Landscape Architect* (1977), 96.

4. Letter in the Alderman Library, University of Virginia, Charlottesville, quoted in Peter Martin, *The Pleasure Gardens of Virginia*, 184.

5. Bernard McMahon, *American Gardener's Calendar* (reprint, 1976), 88, 77.

6. Elizabeth McLean, "Town and Country Gardens in Eighteenth-Century Philadelphia" (1983), 143, PL. 23.

7. Quoted in Edward J. Nygren, *Views and Visions* (1986), 39.

8. Washington Irving, *The Sketchbook of Geoffrey Crayon* (reprint, 1860), 12.

9. Edmund Burke, *Philosophical Enquiry into the Origin of Our Ideas of the Sublime and the Beautiful* (1757); Archibald Alison, *Essays on the Nature and Principles of Taste* (1790); William Gilpin, *Three Essays on Picturesque Beauty* (1791); and the essays of Uvedale Price and Richard Payne Knight.

10. William L. Beiswanger, "The Temple in the Garden" (1983), 170.

11. See S. Allen Chambers, Jr., *Poplar Forest and Thomas Jefferson* (1993), 51–53, and William Howard Adams, *Jefferson's Monticello* (1983), 157–59.

12. Benjamin Henry Latrobe, *The Journal of Latrobe* (1905), 52.

13. Fiske Kimball, "An American Gardener of the Old School" (1925), 74.

14. See Elizabeth P. McLean, *An Overview of the Landscape and Gardens at the Highlands* (1990), 4–9.

15. Lockwood, *Gardens of Colony and State,* vol. 1: 163.

16. Irving B. Eventworth, "Dependencies of the Old-Fashioned House" (1922), 10.

17. See John Michael Vlach, *Back of the Big House* (1993), 70, 71, 87, 95.

18. Latrobe, *Journal*, 23.

19. Edith Tunis Sale, ed., *Historic Gardens of Virginia* (1923), 158–59.

20. Diane Newberry, "Charles Willson Peale and His Garden at Belfield" (1996), 43.

21. Lillian B. Miller, ed., *The Selected Papers of Charles Willson Peale and His Family* (1988), vol. 2: 392–93.

22. Ibid., 390.

23. Susan Stein, *The Worlds of Thomas Jefferson at Monticello* (1993), 280.

24. Quoted in Vlach, *Back of the Big House*, 232.

ARCADIAN VISIONS, 1810–1840

1. "Remarks on the Progress and Present State of the Fine Arts in the United States," quoted in Talbot Hamlin, *Greek Revival Architecture in America* (1944), 320.

2. Quoted in Alan Gowans, *Styles and Types of North American Architecture* (1992), 114.

3. John Warner Barber, *Historical Collections of the State of New Jersey* (1845), 403.

4. Information on "D'Evereux" courtesy of Mimi Miller, Historic Natchez Foundation.

5. The house was torn down; the birdhouse is in a private collection.

6. Lockwood, *Gardens of Colony and State*, vol. 1: 237.

7. Sale, *Historic Gardens of Virginia*, 315, 299.

8. John Warner Barber, *Connecticut Historical Collections* (1836), 23.

9. *History of the Connecticut Valley in Massachusetts* (1879), vol. 1: 285.

10. Ibid., vol. 2: 614, and Mary Plant Spivy, "Gardens in Nineteenth Century Deerfield; a Rabbit's Eye View of the Street" (1975).

11. Margaret Fuller, *Summer on the Lakes, in 1843* (1991), 4, 41, 25, 37.

12. John Warner Barber and Henry B. Howe, *All the Western States and Territories* (1867), 89–90.

13. Lockwood, *Gardens of Colony and State*, vol. 1: 411.

14. See Robert K. Sutton, *Americans Interpret the Parthenon* (1992).

15. Such a pigeon house can be seen in an 1863 photograph of backyards in Little Rock, Arkansas. C. Allan Brown and William Lake Douglas, *A Garden Heritage: The Arkansas Territorial Restoration* (1983), 14.

16. Ibid., 6.

17. Ibid., 10.

18. G. M., "The Fine Arts" (1812), 19.

19. Barber, *Connecticut Historical Collections*, 63–64.

20. Timothy Dwight, *Travels in New-England and New-York* (reprint, 1969), vol. 3: 249–51.

21. Gilpin, *Three Essays on Picturesque Beauty*, 46.

22. Theodore Dwight, *The Northern Traveller* (1841), 102–3.

23. See Debra Lynne Clyde, "Crayonesque Aesthetics in Prose and Architecture" (1986), 154

24. Washington Irving, *The Letters of Washington Irving* (1982) vol 2: 925, 940.

25. Ibid., vol. 3: 133.

26. T. Addison Richards, "Sunnyside" (1856), 9.

27. See Joseph T. Butler, *Sleepy Hollow Restorations* (1983), 42–43. The drawing for the bench is in the collection of the New York Public Library.

Picturesque Gardens *and* Rustic Seats, 1840–1870

1. "The Simple Rural Cottage" (1846), 107.

2. "Some Remarks on the Landscape Art" (1849), 18.

3. "A Visit to Montgomery Place" (1847), 157–59.

4. T. Addison Richards, "Idlewild" (1858), 151.

5. Andrew Jackson Downing, *A Treatise on the Theory and Practice of Landscape Gardening* (reprint, 1977), 294.

6. Downing, *Treatise*, 394, and *The Architecture of Country Houses* (reprint, 1968), 79.

7. Quoted in "The Color of Buildings in Rural Scenery" (1852), 15.

8. "The Home of the Late A. J. Downing" (1853), 23–25.

9. Downing, *Treatise*, 41.

10. Downing, *Treatise*, 393, and Elizabeth P. McLean, *An Overview of the Landscape and Gardens at the Highlands*, 13.

11. Fort Washington, Pennsylvania. The Highlands Historical Society. Diaries of Mrs. George Sheaff.

12. Quoted in Fredrika Bremer, *The Homes of the New World: Impressions of America* (1853), vol. 1: 46.

13. George Jacques, "Landscape Gardening in New England" (1852), 33.

14. "Summary of Historical Data: William Wheelwright Place," Washington, D.C. Library of Congress, Historic American Buildings Survey, and Rev. John Webster Dodge, *William Wheelwright: His Life and Work* (1899), 10.

15. Claude M. Fuess, *The Life of Caleb Cushing* (1923), and Margaret Cushing, "The Cushing Garden," 1924.

16. John Mead Howells, *The Architectural Heritage of The Merrimack* (1941) includes photographs and plans of many Newburyport gardens.

17. See *Alexander Hamilton Ladd Garden Diary* (1995).

18. Sale, *Historic Gardens of Virginia*, 146–47, 125–26.

19. Roberta Seawall Brandau, *History of the Homes and Gardens of Tennessee* (1936), 156–57.

20. Brown and Douglas, *A Garden Heritage*, 16.

21. Washington Irving, *Rocky Mountains* (1837), 21.

22. Susan Davis Price, *Minnesota Gardens* (1995), 37–38.

23. "Letter to the editor," 2, and "Plan of a Garden" (1851), 22, both *The Cultivator* 8.

24. Walter Elder, *The Cottage Garden of America* (1856).

25. Quoted in Fred W. Peterson, "Vernacular Building and Victorian Architecture," in Dell Upton, ed., *Common Places: Readings in American Vernacular Architecture* (1986), 438.

26. Lewis F. Allen, *Rural Architecture* (1853), 111.

27. Emily M. K. Polasek, *A Bohemian Girl in America* (1982), 80.

28. Quoted in T. F. Hamlin, *Greek Revival Architecture in America* (1944), 325.

29. M. Christine Doell, *Gardens of the Gilded Age* (1986), 134.

30. See Susan Bartlett Weber, *Justin Smith Morrill Homestead* (1993).

31. Henry Chandler Bowen, *Papers Pertaining to Landscaping* (n.d.).

32. The manuals were *Love and Parentage Applied to the Improvement of Offspring* and *Evils and Remedies of Excessive and Perverted Sexuality*, both going through forty printings. The 1853 edition of *A Home for All* included advice on building in concrete.

33. Information courtesy of Mimi Miller, Historic Natchez Foundation.

34. Tom Girvan Aikman, *Boss Gardener: The Life and Times of John McLaren* (1988), 40.

35. Diary entry for June 25, 1874, John McLaren Collection, San Francisco Public Library History Room.

36. "Arbor Villa: the Home of Mr. and Mrs. F. M. Smith, East Oakland, California, 1902," photograph album, Berkeley California, Bancroft Library.

37. See Alan Emmett, *So Fine a Prospect* (1996), 125.

Domestic Nostalgia *and* Suburban Comfort, 1870–1900

1. Gillian Brown, *Domestic Individualism* (1990), 173, 191.

2. "Architectural Design," *California Architect and Building News* (1880), 27.

3. *History of the Connecticut Valley in Massachusetts,* vol. 1: 386.

4. Information courtesy of Mary Novak, "Spottswoode."

5. Courtesy of Martin Meek, Enoree, South Carolina.

6. "A Garden on Lake Worth" (1892), 2.

7. "Nature and the Rich" (1894), 251.

8. Clarence Cook, "Beds and Tables" (1876), 813.

9. Anna Gilman Hill, *Forty Years of Gardening* (1938), 270.

10. Sarah Bixby Smith, *Adobe Days* (1987), 8–9.

11. Ibid., 69.

12. Ella Rodman Church, *The Home Garden* (1881), 13.

13. See May Brawley Hill, *Grandmother's Garden* (1995).

14. "An Appropriate Decoration" (1892), 26.

15. Ann Novotny, *Alice's World* (1976), 38.

16. J. B. Harrison, "The Abandoned Farms of New Hampshire" (1899), 573.

17. Candace Wheeler, *Household Art* (1893), 14.

18. Karal Ann Marling, *George Washington Slept Here* (1988), 153.

19. Alice Morse Earle, *Home Life in Colonial Days* (1898), 442–44.

20. Catherine Boisseau, "Mabel Osgood Wright—A 'Natural'" (1983), 25. Wright's nature and garden photographs are in the collection of the Fairfield Historical Society, Fairfield, Connecticut.

21. Gwynn Cochran Prideaux, *Summerhouses of Virginia* (1976), 114.

22. "Hints and Designs for Rustic Buildings" (1848), 363, and "An Amateur, A Few Words on Rustic Arbors" (1850), 320.

23. "Rustic Work for the Lawn" (1895), 75.

24. "The Rustic Touch in the Garden" (1901), 23.

25. Photographs of the house and grounds in the 1890s are in the collection of the Connecticut Valley Historical Museum, Springfield, Massachusetts.

26. L. H. Bailey, "John Burroughs at Home" (1903), 3.

27. Albert Bigelow Paine, *Mark Twain: A Biography* (1922), 508. Twain's study was moved to the Elmira College campus in 1952 and can be visited.

28. Ibid., 522.

29. Phebe Westcott Humphreys, *The Practical Book of Garden Architecture* (1914), 67.

30. Margaret Kittle Boyd, *Reminiscences of Early Marin County Gardens* (1934), n.p.

31. Faith Andrews Bedford, *Frank W. Benson* (1989), 37.

Arts *and* Crafts *and the* Colonial Revival, 1900–1930

1. "The Colonial Renaissance" (1916), 3.

2. Charles Keeler, *The Simple Home* (reprint, 1979) 15, and Charles Wagner, *The Simple Life* (1904), 141.

3. Mary H. Northend, *Remodeled Farmhouses* (1915), 1.

4. Caroline P. Atkinson, ed., *Letters of Susan Hale* (1918), XIV-XV.

5. Annabel Morris Buchanan, "Quaint Beauty in Old-Time Gardens" (1929), 21, and George Alfred Willliams, "New England Gardens" (1924), 14.

6. Julia Cummins, *My Garden Comes of Age* (1926), 4, 109.

7. Ibid., 5, 13.

8. Ibid., 78.

9. Alice Morse Earle, *Old Time Gardens* (1901), 66.

10. Alfred Morton Githens, "The Farmhouse Reclaimed I" (1910), 217.

11. Jessie Peabody Frothingham, *Success in Gardening* (1913), 10.

12. "Salem: Its Houses, Its Streets and Its Gardens Rich with the Atmosphere of Romance and Tradition" (1913), 44.

13. Irving J. Gill, "The Home of the Future: The New Architecture of the West" (1916), 140.

14. Ann Brewster Clarke, *Wade Hampton Pipes: Arts and Crafts Architect in Portland Oregon* (1985), 32.

15. "A House that has the Quality of an Old Homestead" (1908), 388, and Clay Lancaster, *The American Bungalow 1880–1930* (1985), 230.

16. W. S. Rogers, *Garden Planning* (1911), 238.

17. "Pergolas: The Most Picturesque and Practical Feature of the Modern Out-Door Life" (1911), 575–80.

18. Grace Tabor, "An adaptable gated arbor" (1930), 576, and E. H. Miles, "Building a Pergola" (1929), 52.

19. Adaline Thompson, "A Woman's Two-Year-Old Hardy Garden from Seed" (1911), 95. See also Dorothy Houghton, *Houston's Forgotten Heritage* (1991), 184–85.

20. Margaret Harmon, "Making the most of your garden" (1929), 585, and H. Rossiter Snyder, "The garden living room" (1929), 173.

21. Frothingham, *Success in Gardening*, 212.

22. Ruth Dean, *The Livable House: Its Garden* (1917), 84, 133.

23. Ibid., 135

24. Hill, *Forty Years of Gardening*, 129.

25. Loring Underwood, *The Garden and Its Accessories* (1907), 12, 93.

26. Humphreys, *The Practical Book of Garden Architecture*, 141.

27. Ernestine Abercrombie Goodman, *The Garden Club of America: History 1913–1938* (1938), 8, 13.

28. Louise Beebe Wilder, *My Garden* (1916), 4, 188.

29. Ibid., 5, 9.

30. See May Brawley Hill, "The Domestic Garden in American

Impressionist Painting" (1997).

31. Rose V. S. Berry, "Lilian Westcott Hale—Her Art" (1927), 64.

32. "Ugly Homes and Bad Morals" (1905), 73.

33. Quoted in William Ayres, *A Poor Sort of Heaven, A Good Sort of Earth* (1983), 32.

34. Mabel Tuke Priestman, *Artistic Homes* (1910), 41.

35. Kathleen A. Foster, *Daniel Garber 1880–1958* (1980), 24.

36. Frances Duncan, "The Gardens of Cornish" (1906), 17.

37. "Letter to Buzz," unidentified newspaper clipping from the 1920s from the Couse Family Archives, courtesy of Virginia Couse Leavitt.

38. Kevin Starr, *Americans and the California Dream 1850–1915* (1973), 267.

Bauhaus *and the* Home Garden, 1930–1960

1. Albert Frey, "A one-room house that measures 16 feet x 20 feet" (1948), 102.

2. Peter Walker, "The Practice of Landscape Architecture in the Postwar United States" (1993), 250.

3. H. Stuart Ortloff and Henry B. Raymore, *New Gardens for Old* (1934), 30, 33–34.

4. Henry B. Aul, *How to Plant your Home Ground* (1953), 43, 15.

5. Joseph E. Howland, *The House Beautiful Book of Gardens and Outdoor Living* (1958), 44.

6. Ibid., 53.

7. See "How to Build an Outdoor Grill" (1947).

8. Thanks to Mrs. Gordon B. Hurlbut.

9. "A city couple's country place" (1947).

10. James M. Fitch and F. F. Rockwell, *Treasury of American Gardens* (1956), 33–35.

11. Ibid., 68–69.

12. See Carson House, Almaden, Santa Clara County, California. Library of Congress, Historic American Buildings Survey Archives.

13. "Wye Plantation in Maryland," and Don Graf, "Fences with a Purpose" (1948).

14. Henry B. Aul, "Seats in the Home Garden" (1945), 35.

15. See Henry B. Raymore, "On the Way from Here to There: Gates and Entrances" (1944).

16. Currie Cabot, "Green Plains" (1947), 111, 138.

17. Louis H. Frohman and Jean Elliot, *A Pictorial Guide to American Gardens* (1960), 173.

18. Ibid., 165, 182, 184.

19. Photograph in Houston Metropolitan Archives, Houston Public Library.

20. Patricia Thorpe, "Planting Between the Lines" (1990), 126.

21. Frohman and Elliot, 209, 149, 89.

22. J. Horace McFarland, *My Growing Garden* (1915), VII, 9.

23. Ibid., 207.

24. J. Horace McFarland, *Memoirs of a Rose Man* (1949), 24.

25. Caroline Foster's notes on building her cottage as well as transcribed interviews with her and with those who knew her are in the archives of "Fosterfields," Morristown, New Jersey.

26. Caroline Foster, who had given "Fosterfields" to the Morris County Park Commission in 1967, died at age 102 in 1979.

Looking Back — The Recent Past

1. See Adrian Higgins, "Tempting Temples" (1992), and David Maurer, "Cultural Exchange" (1995).

2. *Beautifying the Home Grounds* (reprinted as *Wonderful Wooden Garden Structures,* 1992), introduction.

3. See Barbara Whitaker, "Why Those Backyards Are Looking Like Versailles" (1966).

4. See Elizabeth H. Hunter, "An Artist's Garden" (1992), and Mia Amato, "Twice Blessed" (1997).

5. See Kenneth Hunt, "Southern Hospitality" (1996).

6. See Barbara H. Seeber, "An Orderly Retreat" (1996).

7. See Jean Creznic, "Choosing and Using the Best" (1989).

8. See Adrienne Cook, "American Country Garden" (1992).

9. See David Maurer, "A Visit to Hillsborough, North Carolina: Montrose" (1995).

10. See Patti Hagan, "A Farm in Flower" (1991).

11. See Marsha L. Larsen, "A Carolina Saltbox" (1987), and Mimi Handler, "The 18th-Century House, c. 1970" (1988).

12. See J. Vivian, "Rustic Furniture Adirondack Style" (1995).

13. See Richard R. Iversen, "Rustic Pleasures" (1994), and Minda Zetlin, "A 19th-Century Romance" (1996).

14. Mary Schroer, "Prairie Gothic" (1996), 67.

15. See "A Garden for All Seasons" (1993), Sharon Abroms, "A Garden Room for Every Mood" (1996), and Penny Vogel, "A Design from the Heart" (1993).

16. See Ken Moore, "Gazing Globes" (1992).

17. Margery Guest, "Up North in Search of a Whirligig" (1994), 6, and Julia H. Thomason, "Fabulous Finds for the Garden" (1994), 94.

18. Leon Whiteson describes the making of his garden in *A Garden Story* (1995).

BIBLIOGRAPHY

Abroms, Sharon. "A Garden Room for Every Mood." *Fine Gardening* 9 (May–June 1996): 59–63.

Adams, William Howard. *Jefferson's Monticello*. New York: Abbeville Press, 1983.

Aikman, Tom Girvan. *Boss Gardener: The Life and Times of John McLaren*. San Francisco: Don't Call it Frisco Press, 1988.

Albaugh, Benjamin F. *The Gardenette or City Backyard Gardening on the Sandwich System*. Cincinnati: privately printed, 1917.

Alexander Hamilton Ladd Garden Diary. Portsmouth, N.H.: National Society of Colonial Dames of America, 1995.

Allen, Gordon. "The Vale." *Old Time New England* 42 (Spring 1952): 81–87.

Allen, Lewis F. *Rural Architecture*. New York: C. M. Saxton, 1853.

Alex, William. *Calvert Vaux, Architect and Planner*. New York: Ink, 1994.

"An Amateur, A Few Words on Rustic Arbors." *The Horticulturist* 4 (January 1850): 320.

Amato, Mia. "Twice Blessed." *House Beautiful* 139 (June 1997): 88–93.

Andrews, Wayne. *American Gothic: Its Origins, Its Trials, Its Triumphs*. New York: Random House, 1975.

"An Appropriate Decoration." *Garden and Forest* 5 (January 20, 1892): 26.

Arbor Villa photograph album. Bancroft Library, University of California. Berkeley, California.

"Architectural Design." *California Architect and Building News* (March 1880): 27.

Asleson, Robyn, and Barbara Moore. *Dialogue with Nature: Landscape and Literature in 19th-Century America*. Washington, D.C.: Corcoran Gallery of Art, 1985.

Atkinson, Caroline P., ed. *Letters of Susan Hale*. Boston: Marshall Jones Company, 1918.

Aul, Henry B. *How to Plant Your Home Ground*. New York: Sheridan House, 1953.

———. *How to Build Garden Structures*. New York: Sheridan House, 1950.

———. "Pergolas and Arches." *The Home Garden* 5 (February 1945): 70–73.

———. "Seats in the Home Garden." *The Home Garden* 5 (February 1945): 32–35.

Ayres, William. *A Poor Sort of Heaven, A Good Sort of Earth, The Rose Valley Arts and Crafts Experiment*. Chadds Ford, Penn.: Brandywine River Museum, 1983.

Bailey, L. H. "John Burroughs at Home." *American Gardening* 14 (January 1903): 1–4.

Balge, Marjorie. "William de Leftwich Dodge: American Renaissance Artist." *Art and Antiques* (January–February 1982): 96–103.

Barber, John Warner. *Connecticut Historical Collections*. New Haven: Durrie, 1836.

———. *Historical Collections of Massachusetts*. Worcester: Lazell, 1846.

———. *Historical Collections of the State of New Jersey*. New York: S. Tuttle, 1845.

———, and Henry Howe. *All the Western States and Territories*. Cincinnati: Henry Howe, 1867.

Barnard, Charles. *A Simple Flower Garden for Country Homes, A Practical Guide for Every Lady*. Boston: Loring, 1870.

Beautifying the Home Grounds. 1926. Reprinted as *Wonderful Wooden Garden Structures*. Hillsborough, N.C.: Hummer Press, 1992.

Bedford, Faith Andrews. *Frank W. Benson*. New York: Berry-Hill Galleries, 1989.

Beecher, Catherine, and Harriet Beecher Stowe. *The American Woman's Home*. New York: J. B. Ford, 1869.

Beevans, Edith Rossiter. "Gardens and Gardening in Early Maryland." *Maryland Historical Magazine* 30 (1950): 243–70.

Beiswanger, William L. "The Temple in the Garden: Thomas Jefferson's Vision of the Monticello Landscape." *Eighteenth Century Life* 8 (January 1983): 170–88.

Benes, Peter, ed. *The Farm*. The Dublin Seminar for New England Folklife Annual Proceedings, 1986. Boston: Boston University, 1988.

Benjamin, Asher. *The American Builder's Companion*. 1814. Reprint, New York: Dover, 1965.

———. *Practice of Architecture Containing the Five Orders of Architecture*. Boston: Asher Benjamin, 1833.

Bentley, The Reverend William. *The Diary of William Bentley, D.D.* 1905. Reprint, Gloucester, Mass.: Peter Smith, 1962.

Berry, Rose V. S. "Lilian Westcott Hale—Her Art." *The American Magazine of Art* 18 (February 1927): 39–70.

Beverly, Robert. *The History and Present State of Virginia*. 1705.

Edited by Louis B. White. Chapel Hill: UNC, 1947.

Birch, William. *The Country Seats of the United States of North America*. Springland, Penn.: William Birch, 1808.

Bivins, John, Jr. *The Moravian Potters in North Carolina*. Chapel Hill: University of North Carolina Press, 1972.

Blanchan, Neltje. *The American Flower Garden*. New York: Doubleday, Page, 1909.

Boisseau, Catherine. "Mabel Osgood Wright—A 'Natural'." *Fairfield Citizen News* (May 25, 1983): 25.

Bowen, Henry Chandler. *Papers Pertaining to Landscaping*. Boston: Society for the Preservation of New England Antiquities, n.d.

Boyd, Margaret Kittle. *Reminiscences of Early Marin County Gardens*. San Francisco: San Francisco Garden Club, 1934.

Brandau, Roberta Seawall. *History of the Homes and Gardens of Tennessee*. Nashville: Parthenon Press, 1936.

Bremer, Fredrika. *The Homes of the New World: Impressions of America*. 2 vols. New York: Harper, 1853.

Brewster, Kate L. *The Little Garden for Little Money*. Boston: The Atlantic Monthly Press, 1924.

Bridgeman, Thomas. *The Young Gardener's Assistant*. New York: A. Hanford, 1844.

Briggs, Loutrel W. *Charleston Gardens*. Columbia: University of South Carolina Press, 1951.

Briggs, Peter M. "Timothy Dwight 'Composes' a Landscape for New England." *American Quarterly* 40 (September 1988): 359–77.

Britz, Billie Sherrill. "The Orangery in England and America." *Antiques* 149 (April 1996): 594–601.

Brooks, Paul. "Birds and Women." *Audubon* 82 (September 1980): 88–97.

Brown, C. Allan, and William Lake Douglas. *A Garden Heritage: The Arkansas Territorial Restoration*. Little Rock: The Arkansas Territorial Restoration Foundation, 1983.

Brown, Gillian. *Domestic Individualism: Imagining Self in Nineteenth-Century America*. Berkeley: University of California Press, 1990.

Buchanan, Annabel Morris. "Quaint Beauty in Old-Time Gardens." *Better Homes and Gardens* 7 (April 1929): 21, 132.

Burchard, John, and Albert Bush-Brown. *The Architecture of America*. Boston: Little, Brown, 1961.

Burton, Kristin. "The Garden of Colonial Flowers at Monroe Tavern." *Garden History* 25 (Summer 1997): 45–58.

Butler, Joseph T. "American mid-Victorian Outdoor Furniture."*Antiques* 75 (January 1959): 564–69.

———. *Sleepy Hollow Restorations*. Tarrytown, N.Y.: Sleepy Hollow Restorations, 1983.

Cabot, Currie. "Green Plains." *Town & Country* 101 (January 1947): 109–13, 138.

Caffin, Charles H. "The Art of Frank W. Benson." *Harper's Monthly* 119 (June 1909): 105–44.

Candee, Richard M. "Strictly for the Birds." *Old Time New England* 56 (Summer 1966): 12–14.

Carter, Edward C., II, ed. *The Virginia Journals of Benjamin Latrobe, 1795–1798*. 2 vols. New Haven: Yale University Press, 1977.

Chambers, S. Allen, Jr. *Poplar Forest and Thomas Jefferson*. Forest, Va.: The Corporation for Poplar Forest, 1993.

Christian, Frances Archer, and Susanne Williams Massie, eds. *Homes and Gardens of Old Virginia*. Richmond: Garrett and Massie, 1931.

Church, Ella Rodman. *The Home Garden*. New York: D. Appleton, 1881.

"A city couple's country place." *House and Garden* 91 (June 1947): 84–85.

Clarke, Ann Brewster. *Wade Hampton Pipes: Arts and Crafts Architect in Portland, Oregon*. Portland: Binford and Mort Publishing, 1985.

Clyde, Debra Lynne. "Crayonesque Aesthetics in Prose and Architecture." Ph.D. diss., Drew University, 1986.

"The Colonial Renaissance." *White Pine Series of Architectural Monographs* 2 (February 1916): 3–14.

"The Color of Buildings in Rural Scenery." *The Horticulturist* 7 (January 1852): 15–17.

Conner, Patrick. *Oriental Architecture in the West*. London: Thames and Hudson, 1979.

Cook, Adrienne. "American Country Garden." *Southern Accents* 15 (February 1992): 74–83.

Cook, Clarence. "Beds and Tables." *Scribner's Magazine* 11 (April 1876): 809–22.

Creznic, Jean. "Choosing and Using the Best." *Early American Life* 20 (April 1989): 18–29.

Cummins, Julia. *My Garden Comes of Age*. New York: Macmillan, 1926.

Cushing, Margaret. "The Cushing Garden, 98 High Street." Typescript. Newburyport, Mass.: Newburyport Historical Society, 1938.

Davidson, Ralph C. *Garden Ornaments and Furniture*. New York: Munn, 1910.

Davis, Jane B. *The Gothic Revival Style in America 1830–1870*. Houston, Tex.: Museum of Fine Arts, 1976.

Dean, Ruth. *The Livable House: Its Garden*. New York: Moffat, Yard, 1917.

Dodge, Reverend John Webster. *William Wheelwright: His Life*

The New Republic, 1780–1810

1. Merrill D. Peterson, ed., *The Portable Thomas Jefferson* (1977), 290.
2. Edward Augustus Kendall, *Travels through the Northern Parts of the United States 1807–1808,* 3 vols. (New York: Riley, 1809) and others. The term first appeared in print in the 1742 second edition of Stephen Switzer's *Iconographic Rustica* (London, 1718). As late as 1827 John Lowell described his estate "Bromley Vale" near Boston as a *ferme ornée.* See Tamara Platkins Thornton, *Cultivating Gentlemen* (1989), 111.
3. Frederick Doveton Nicholas and Ralph E. Griswold, *Thomas Jefferson Landscape Architect* (1977), 96.
4. Letter in the Alderman Library, University of Virginia, Charlottesville, quoted in Peter Martin, *The Pleasure Gardens of Virginia*, 184.
5. Bernard McMahon, *American Gardener's Calendar* (reprint, 1976), 88, 77.
6. Elizabeth McLean, "Town and Country Gardens in Eighteenth-Century Philadelphia" (1983), 143, PL. 23.
7. Quoted in Edward J. Nygren, *Views and Visions* (1986), 39.
8. Washington Irving, *The Sketchbook of Geoffrey Crayon* (reprint, 1860), 12.
9. Edmund Burke, *Philosophical Enquiry into the Origin of Our Ideas of the Sublime and the Beautiful* (1757); Archibald Alison, *Essays on the Nature and Principles of Taste* (1790); William Gilpin, *Three Essays on Picturesque Beauty* (1791); and the essays of Uvedale Price and Richard Payne Knight.
10. William L. Beiswanger, "The Temple in the Garden" (1983), 170.
11. See S. Allen Chambers, Jr., *Poplar Forest and Thomas Jefferson* (1993), 51–53, and William Howard Adams, *Jefferson's Monticello* (1983), 157–59.
12. Benjamin Henry Latrobe, *The Journal of Latrobe* (1905), 52.
13. Fiske Kimball, "An American Gardener of the Old School" (1925), 74.
14. See Elizabeth P. McLean, *An Overview of the Landscape and Gardens at the Highlands* (1990), 4–9.
15. Lockwood, *Gardens of Colony and State,* vol. 1: 163.
16. Irving B. Eventworth, "Dependencies of the Old-Fashioned House" (1922), 10.
17. See John Michael Vlach, *Back of the Big House* (1993), 70, 71, 87, 95.
18. Latrobe, *Journal*, 23.
19. Edith Tunis Sale, ed., *Historic Gardens of Virginia* (1923), 158–59.
20. Diane Newberry, "Charles Willson Peale and His Garden at Belfield" (1996), 43.
21. Lillian B. Miller, ed., *The Selected Papers of Charles Willson Peale and His Family* (1988), vol. 2: 392–93.
22. Ibid., 390.
23. Susan Stein, *The Worlds of Thomas Jefferson at Monticello* (1993), 280.
24. Quoted in Vlach, *Back of the Big House*, 232.

Arcadian Visions, 1810–1840

1. "Remarks on the Progress and Present State of the Fine Arts in the United States," quoted in Talbot Hamlin, *Greek Revival Architecture in America* (1944), 320.
2. Quoted in Alan Gowans, *Styles and Types of North American Architecture* (1992), 114.
3. John Warner Barber, *Historical Collections of the State of New Jersey* (1845), 403.
4. Information on "D'Evereux" courtesy of Mimi Miller, Historic Natchez Foundation.
5. The house was torn down; the birdhouse is in a private collection.
6. Lockwood, *Gardens of Colony and State*, vol. 1: 237.
7. Sale, *Historic Gardens of Virginia*, 315, 299.
8. John Warner Barber, *Connecticut Historical Collections* (1836), 23.
9. *History of the Connecticut Valley in Massachusetts* (1879), vol. 1: 285.
10. Ibid., vol. 2: 614, and Mary Plant Spivy, "Gardens in Nineteenth Century Deerfield; a Rabbit's Eye View of the Street" (1975).
11. Margaret Fuller, *Summer on the Lakes, in 1843* (1991), 4, 41, 25, 37.
12. John Warner Barber and Henry B. Howe, *All the Western States and Territories* (1867), 89–90.
13. Lockwood, *Gardens of Colony and State*, vol. 1: 411.
14. See Robert K. Sutton, *Americans Interpret the Parthenon* (1992).
15. Such a pigeon house can be seen in an 1863 photograph of backyards in Little Rock, Arkansas. C. Allan Brown and William Lake Douglas, *A Garden Heritage: The Arkansas Territorial Restoration* (1983), 14.
16. Ibid., 6.
17. Ibid., 10.
18. G. M., "The Fine Arts" (1812), 19.
19. Barber, *Connecticut Historical Collections*, 63–64.
20. Timothy Dwight, *Travels in New-England and New-York* (reprint, 1969), vol. 3: 249–51.

21. Gilpin, *Three Essays on Picturesque Beauty*, 46.

22. Theodore Dwight, *The Northern Traveller* (1841), 102–3.

23. See Debra Lynne Clyde, "Crayonesque Aesthetics in Prose and Architecture" (1986), 154

24. Washington Irving, *The Letters of Washington Irving* (1982) vol 2: 925, 940.

25. Ibid., vol. 3: 133.

26. T. Addison Richards, "Sunnyside" (1856), 9.

27. See Joseph T. Butler, *Sleepy Hollow Restorations* (1983), 42–43. The drawing for the bench is in the collection of the New York Public Library.

Picturesque Gardens *and* Rustic Seats, 1840–1870

1. "The Simple Rural Cottage" (1846), 107.

2. "Some Remarks on the Landscape Art" (1849), 18.

3. "A Visit to Montgomery Place" (1847), 157–59.

4. T. Addison Richards, "Idlewild" (1858), 151.

5. Andrew Jackson Downing, *A Treatise on the Theory and Practice of Landscape Gardening* (reprint, 1977), 294.

6. Downing, *Treatise*, 394, and *The Architecture of Country Houses* (reprint, 1968), 79.

7. Quoted in "The Color of Buildings in Rural Scenery" (1852), 15.

8. "The Home of the Late A. J. Downing" (1853), 23–25.

9. Downing, *Treatise*, 41.

10. Downing, *Treatise*, 393, and Elizabeth P. McLean, *An Overview of the Landscape and Gardens at the Highlands*, 13.

11. Fort Washington, Pennsylvania. The Highlands Historical Society. Diaries of Mrs. George Sheaff.

12. Quoted in Fredrika Bremer, *The Homes of the New World: Impressions of America* (1853), vol. 1: 46.

13. George Jacques, "Landscape Gardening in New England" (1852), 33.

14. "Summary of Historical Data: William Wheelwright Place," Washington, D.C. Library of Congress, Historic American Buildings Survey, and Rev. John Webster Dodge, *William Wheelwright: His Life and Work* (1899), 10.

15. Claude M. Fuess, *The Life of Caleb Cushing* (1923), and Margaret Cushing, "The Cushing Garden," 1924.

16. John Mead Howells, *The Architectural Heritage of The Merrimack* (1941) includes photographs and plans of many Newburyport gardens.

17. See *Alexander Hamilton Ladd Garden Diary* (1995).

18. Sale, *Historic Gardens of Virginia*, 146–47, 125–26.

19. Roberta Seawall Brandau, *History of the Homes and Gardens of Tennessee* (1936), 156–57.

20. Brown and Douglas, *A Garden Heritage*, 16.

21. Washington Irving, *Rocky Mountains* (1837), 21.

22. Susan Davis Price, *Minnesota Gardens* (1995), 37–38.

23. "Letter to the editor," 2, and "Plan of a Garden" (1851), 22, both *The Cultivator* 8.

24. Walter Elder, *The Cottage Garden of America* (1856).

25. Quoted in Fred W. Peterson, "Vernacular Building and Victorian Architecture," in Dell Upton, ed., *Common Places: Readings in American Vernacular Architecture* (1986), 438.

26. Lewis F. Allen, *Rural Architecture* (1853), 111.

27. Emily M. K. Polasek, *A Bohemian Girl in America* (1982), 80.

28. Quoted in T. F. Hamlin, *Greek Revival Architecture in America* (1944), 325.

29. M. Christine Doell, *Gardens of the Gilded Age* (1986), 134.

30. See Susan Bartlett Weber, *Justin Smith Morrill Homestead* (1993).

31. Henry Chandler Bowen, *Papers Pertaining to Landscaping* (n.d.).

32. The manuals were *Love and Parentage Applied to the Improvement of Offspring* and *Evils and Remedies of Excessive and Perverted Sexuality*, both going through forty printings. The 1853 edition of *A Home for All* included advice on building in concrete.

33. Information courtesy of Mimi Miller, Historic Natchez Foundation.

34. Tom Girvan Aikman, *Boss Gardener: The Life and Times of John McLaren* (1988), 40.

35. Diary entry for June 25, 1874, John McLaren Collection, San Francisco Public Library History Room.

36. "Arbor Villa: the Home of Mr. and Mrs. F. M. Smith, East Oakland, California, 1902," photograph album, Berkeley California, Bancroft Library.

37. See Alan Emmett, *So Fine a Prospect* (1996), 125.

Domestic Nostalgia *and* Suburban Comfort, 1870–1900

1. Gillian Brown, *Domestic Individualism* (1990), 173, 191.

2. "Architectural Design," *California Architect and Building News* (1880), 27.

3. *History of the Connecticut Valley in Massachusetts*, vol. 1: 386.

4. Information courtesy of Mary Novak, "Spottswoode."

and Work. Cambridge: Cambridge University Press, 1899.

Doell, M. Christine. *Gardens of the Gilded Age*. Syracuse, N.Y.: Syracuse University Press, 1986.

Downing, Andrew Jackson. *The Architecture of Country Houses*. 1850. Reprint, New York: DeCapo Press, 1968.

———. *Cottage Residences*. 1842. Reprint, New York: Dover, 1981.

———. *Rural Essays*. New York: George Putnam, 1853.

———. *A Treatise on the Theory and Practice of Landscape Gardening Adapted to North America*. 1841. Reprint, New York: Theophrastus Press, 1977.

Downing, Antoinette Forrester. *Early Homes of Rhode Island*. Richmond, Va.: Garrett and Massie, 1937.

Dugmore, A. R. *Bird Homes*. New York: Doubleday, McClure, 1900.

Duncan, Frances. "The Gardens of Cornish." *Century Magazine* 72 (May 1906): 3–19.

Dwight, Theodore. *The Northern Traveller*, 6th ed. New York: John Haven, 1841.

Dwight, Timothy. *Travels in New-England and New-York*. 4 vols. 1821. Reprint, Cambridge, Mass.: Harvard University Press, 1969.

Earle, Alice Morse. *Home Life in Colonial Days*. New York: Macmillan and Co., 1898.

———. *Old Time Gardens*. New York: Macmillan and Co., 1901.

Eberlein, Harold Donaldson. *The Practical Book of Garden Structure and Design*. Philadelphia: J. S. Lippincott, 1937.

Elder, Paul, ed. *The Architecture and Landscape Gardening of the Exposition*. San Francisco: P. Elder, 1915.

Elder, Walter. *The Cottage Garden of America*, 2nd ed. Philadelphia: Moss and Brother, 1856.

Emmett, Alan. *So Fine a Prospect: Historic New England Gardens*. Hanover, N.H.: University Press of New England, 1996.

Eventworth, Irving B. "Dependencies of the Old-Fashioned House." *The White Pine Series of Architectural Monographs* 8 (April 1922): 3–13.

Fales, Dean A., Jr. "Joseph Berrell's Pleasant Hill." *Transactions of The Colonial Society of Massachussets* 43 (1960): 373–90.

Faris, John T. *Old Gardens in and about Philadelphia*. Indianapolis: Bobbs-Merrill, 1932.

Farwell, Elizabeth Foster. *My Garden Gate is on the Latch*. Chicago: La Salle Street Press, 1962.

Feltwell, John, and Neil Odenwald. *Live Oak Splendor: Gardens along the Mississippi*. Dallas: Taylor Publishing Company, 1992.

Fessenden, Thomas Green. *The New American Gardener*. Boston: J. B. Russell, 1828.

Fitch, James M., and F. F. Rockwell. *Treasury of American Gardens*.

New York: Harper & Brothers, 1956.

Forman, H. Chandlee. *Old Buildings, Gardens and Furniture in Tidewater Maryland*. Cambridge, Md.: Tidewater Publishers, 1967.

———. *Tidewater Maryland Architecture and Gardens*. New York: Architectural Book Publishing, 1956.

Foster, Kathleen A. *Daniel Garber 1880–1958*. Philadelphia: Pennsylvania Academy of the Fine Arts, 1980.

Frey, Albert. "A one-room house that measures 16 feet x 20 feet." *House and Garden* 92 (January 1948): 92–93, 102.

Frohman, Louis H., and Jean Elliot. *A Pictorial Guide to American Gardens*. New York: Crown, 1960.

Frothingham, Jessie Peabody. *Success in Gardening*. New York: Duffield, 1913.

Fuess, Claude M. *The Life of Caleb Cushing*. New York: Harcourt, Brace, 1923.

Fuller, Margaret. *Summer on the Lakes, in 1843*. Chicago: University of Illinois Press, 1991.

G. M. "The Fine Arts." *Port Folio* 8 (July 1812): 19.

"A Garden for All Seasons." *Country Living* 16 (April 1993): 124–31.

"Garden Furniture." *The Horticulturist* 8 (July 1853): 301–4.

"A Garden on Lake Worth." *The Tropical Sun* (June 23, 1892): 2.

Gill, Irving J. "The Home of the Future: The New Architecture of the West." *Craftsman* 30 (May 1916): 140–51.

Gilpin, William. *Three Essays on Picturesque Beauty*. London: R. Blamire, 1791.

Giroud, Mark. *Sweetness and Light: The Queen Anne Movement 1860–1900*. New Haven: Yale University Press, 1984.

Githens, Alfred Morton. "The Farmhouse Reclaimed I." *House and Garden* 17 (June 1910): 217.

Goodman, Ernestine Abercrombie. *The Garden Club of America: History 1913–1938*. Philadelphia: privately printed, 1938.

Gottesman, Rita Susswein. *The Arts and Crafts in New York 1726–1776*. New York: The New-York Historical Society, 1938.

Gowans, Alan. *Styles and Types of North American Architecture*. New York: HarperCollins, 1992.

Graf, Don. "Fences with a Purpose." *House and Garden* 93 (May 1948): 124–25.

Grant, Anne. *Memoirs of an American Lady*. 1808. American ed., Albany: Joel Munsell, 1876.

Grantham, Shelby. "Sarah Goodwin's Garden." *Early American Life* 20 (February 1929): 50–57.

Griffith, Mary S. *Gardening on Nothing a Year*. Boston: Hale, Cushman and Flint, 1937.

Griswold, Mac, and Eleanor Weller. *The Golden Age of American*

Gardens. New York: Harry N. Abrams, 1992.

Griswold, Ralph E. "Early American Garden Houses." *Antiques* 98 (July 1970): 82–87.

Guest, Margery. "Up North in Search of a Whirligig." *American Horticulturist* 73 (August 1994): 6–7.

Hagan, Patti. "A Farm in Flower." *House and Garden* 163 (May 1991): 117–23, 193.

Hageman, Jane Sikes. *Ohio Pioneer Artists*. Cincinnati: Ohio Furniture Makers, 1993.

Halsted, Byron David. *Barn Plans and Outbuildings*. New York: O. Judd, 1881.

Hamlin, Talbot. *Greek Revival Architecture in America*. New York: Oxford University Press, 1944.

Handler, Mimi. "The 18th-Century House, c. 1970." *Early American Life* 19 (February 1988): 26–35.

Harmon, Margaret. "Making the most of your garden." *The American Home* 3 (August 1929): 585, 652.

Harrison, J. B. "The Abandoned Farms of New Hampshire." *Garden and Forest* 10 (November 27, 1899): 573–74.

Harrison, Peter Joel. *Fences*. Richmond, Va.: Dietz Press, 1993.

———. *Gazebos*. Richmond, Va.: Dietz Press, 1995.

Hedrick, U. P. *A History of Horticulture in America to 1860*. Reprint, Portland, Ore.: Timber Press, 1988.

Henderson, Charles. *Henderson's Picturesque Gardens and Ornamental Gardening Illustrated*. New York: P. Henderson, 1908.

Henderson, Peter. *Gardening for Pleasure*. New York: O. Judd, 1887.

Hershey, George L. *High Victorian Gothic: A Study in Associationism*. Baltimore: Johns Hopkins University Press, 1972.

Higgins, Adrian. "Tempting Temples." *Garden Design* 11 (May–June 1992): 10–11.

Higgins, Charles Arthur. "Mary Harrod Northend." *Massachussetts Magazine* 8 (January 1915): 23–26.

Higginson, Francis. *New Englands Plantation*. Massachusetts Historical Society Proceedings, vol. 62. Boston: Massachussetts Historical Society, 1929.

Higham, John. *Strangers in the Land: Patterns of American Nationalism 1880–1925*. New York: Atheneum, 1985.

Hill, Anna Gillman. *Forty Years of Gardening*. New York: Frederick Stokes, 1938.

Hill, May Brawley. "The Domestic Garden In American Impressionist Painting." Lisa N. Peters and Peter M. Lukehart, eds. *Visions of Home*. Carlisle, Penn.: The Trout Gallery, Dickinson College, 1997.

———. *Grandmother's Garden: The Old-Fashioned American Garden 1865–1915*. New York: Harry N. Abrams, 1995.

"Hints and Designs for Rustic Buildings." *The Horticulturist* 2 (February 1848): 363–65.

History of the Connecticut Valley in Massachusetts. 2 vols. Philadelphia: Louis H. Everts, 1879.

Holtzoper, E. C. "Garden Accessories." *Country Life in America* 8 (September 1905): 523–26.

"The Home of the Late A. J. Downing." *The Horticulturist* 8 (January 1853): 20–27.

Hooper, Charles Edward. *The Country House*. Garden City: Doubleday, Page, 1913.

———. *Reclaiming the Old House*, New York: McBride, Nast, 1913.

Houghton, Dorthy Knox Howe, et al. *Houston's Forgotten Heritage*. Houston, Tex.: Rice University Press, 1991.

House and Garden's New Complete Book of Gardens. New York: Simon and Schuster, 1995.

"A House that has the Quality of an Old Homestead." *Craftsman* 14 (April 1908): 388–94.

"How Pergolas Add to the Appreciation and Enjoyment of Outdoor Life." *Craftsman* 17 (November 1907): 202.

"How to Build an Outdoor Grill." *House and Garden* 91 (June 1947): 150.

Howe, Katherine S. "Product of an Age: The Gothic Revival in the United States." *Nineteenth Century* 3 (Spring 1977): 62–71.

Howells, John Mead. *The Architectural Heritage of The Merrimack*. New York: Architectural Book Publishing, 1941.

Howett, Catherine. "Crying Taste in the Wilderness: Disciples of A. J. Downing in Georgia." *Landscape Journal* 1 (Spring 1982): 19–22.

Howland, Joseph E. *The House Beautiful Book of Gardens and Outdoor Living*. New York: Doubleday, 1958.

Humphreys, Phebe Westcott. *The Practical Book of Garden Architecture*. Philadelphia: J. B. Lippincott Co., 1914.

Hunt, Kenneth. "Southern Hospitality." *Colonial Homes* 22 (Febuary 1996): 82–87.

Hunter, Elizabeth H. "An Artist's Garden." *House Beautiful* 129 (May 1992): 84–88.

Irving, Washington. *The Letters of Washington Irving*. 3 vols. Boston: Twayne, 1982.

———. *Rocky Mountains*. 2 vols. Philadelphia: Carey, Lea and Blanchard, 1837.

———. *The Sketchbook of Geoffrey Crayon*. 1819. Reprint, New York: A. L. Burt, 1860.

Iverson, Richard R. "Rustic Pleasures." *American Horticulturist* 73 (October 1994): 30–33.

Jackson, Kenneth T. *Crabgrass Frontier: The Suburbanization of the United States*. New York: Oxford University Press, 1985.

Jacques, George. "Landscape Gardening in New England." *The Horticulturist* 7 (January 1852): 33–37.

Jennings, Jan. *American Vernacular Design 1870–1940*. Ames, Ia.: Iowa State University Press, 1988.

Jordy, William H. *American Buildings and Their Architects: Progressive and Academic Styles at the Turn of the Century*. New York: Doubleday, 1972.

————. *The Impact of European Modernism in the Mid-Twentieth Century*. New York: Oxford University Press, 1972.

Kamerling, Bruce. *Irving J. Gill, Architect*. San Diego, Calif.: San Diego Historical Society, 1993.

Karn, J. M. *Practical Landscape Gardening*. Cincinnati: Moore, Wilstack, Keys, 1855.

Kassler, Elizabeth B. *Modern Gardens and the Landscape*. New York: The Museum of Modern Art, 1964.

Keeler, Charles. *The Simple Home*. 1904. Reprint, Santa Barbara: Peregrine Smith, 1979.

Kellar, Herbert Anthony, ed. *Solon Robertson: Pioneer and Agriculturist, Selected Writings*. Indianapolis: Indiana Historical Bureau, 1936.

Kennedy, Roger. *Architecture, Men, Women, and Money*. New York: Random House, 1983.

Kimball, Fiske. "A Landscape Garden on the James in 1793." *Landscape Architecture* 45 (January 1924): 123.

————. "An American Gardener of the Old School—George Heussler (1751–1817)." *Landscape Architecture* 47 (January 1925): 71–75.

Kimball, Mary G. "The Revival of the Colonial." *Architectural Record* 62 (July 1927): 1–17.

Kirker, Harold. *California's Architectural Frontier: Style and Tradition in the Nineteenth Century*. San Marino, Calif.: The Huntington Library, 1960.

Kunst, Scott. "Post-Victorian Landscapes and Gardens." *Old-House Journal* 14 (April 1986): 128–35.

————. "Sitting Outside 1865–1940." *Old-House Journal* 21 (July–August 1993): 20–22.

Ladd, Alexander H. *Garden Book 1888–1895*. Ruthanne C. Rogers and Virginia P. Chisholm, eds. Portsmouth, N.H.: The National Society of The Colonial Dames in the State of New Hampshire, 1996.

Lamb, Martha J. *The Homes of Americans*. New York: Appleton and Company, 1879.

Lancaster, Clay. *The American Bungalow 1880–1930*. New York: Abbeville Press, 1985.

Larsen, Marsha L. "A Carolina Saltbox." *Early American Life* 18 (April 1987): 50–59.

Latrobe, Benjamin Henry. *The Journal of Latrobe*. New York: D. Appleton, 1905.

Law, Margaret Lathrop. "The Highlands." *House Beautiful* 70 (August 1931): 148–51, 164–65.

Leuchars, R. B. "Notes on Gardens and Gardening in the Neighborhood of Boston." *Magazine of Horticulture* 16 (February 1850): 49–60.

Lockwood, Alice B., ed. *Gardens of Colony and State*. 2 vols. New York: Charles Scribner's Sons for the Garden Club of America, 1931.

Long, Elias A. *Ornamental Gardening for Americans*. New York: Orange Judd, 1885.

Lossing, Benson J. *The Hudson from the Wilderness to the Sea*. Troy, N.Y.: H. B. Nims, 1866.

Loth, Calder, and Julius Trousdale Sadler, Jr. *The Only Proper Style: Gothic Architecture in America*. Boston: New York Graphic Society, 1975.

Lowell, Guy. *American Gardens*. Boston: Bates and Guild Co., 1902.

Lynn, Catherine. *Wallpaper in America*. New York: W.W. Norton, 1980.

Maccubbin, R. P., and Peter Martin, eds. *British and American Gardens in the Eighteenth Century*. Williamsburg, Va.: Colonial Williamsburg, 1984.

MacDougall, Elizabeth Blair, ed. *Prophet with Honor: The Career of Andrew Jackson Downing 1815–1852*. Washington, D. C.: Dumbarton Oaks, 1989.

Marling, Karal Ann. *George Washington Slept Here: Colonial Revivals and American Culture, 1876–1986*. Cambridge, Mass.: Harvard University Press, 1988.

Martin, George A. *Fences, Gates and Bridges*. New York: O. Judd, 1887.

Martin, Peter. *The Pleasure Gardens of Virginia from Jamestown to Jefferson*. Princeton: Princeton University Press, 1991.

Martin, Ralph de. "Homes of American Artists: An Artist's Home in Rose Valley." *American Homes and Gardens* 6 (March 1909): 95–98.

Matusik, Joe-Ellen. "Period Garden Plans." *Old-House Journal* 24 (March–April 1996): 28–31.

Maurer, David. "Cultural Exchanges." *Classic Home* 2 (Spring 1995): 54–61.

————. "A Visit to Hillsborough, North Carolina: Montrose." *Colonial Homes* 21 (April 1995): 74–75.

McFarland, J. Horace. *Memoirs of a Rose Man: Tales from Breeze Hill*. Emmaus, Penn.: Rodale Press, 1949.

————. *My Growing Garden*. New York: Macmillan, 1915.

McLaren, John. Diary. San Francisco Public Library History Room. San Francisco, Calif.

McLean, Elizabeth P. "Town and Country Gardens in Eighteenth Century Philadelphia." *Eighteenth Century Life* 8 (January 1983): 136–47.

———. *An Overview of the Landscape and Gardens at the Highlands*. Fort Washington, Penn.: The Highlands Historical Society, 1990.

McMahon, Bernard. *American Gardener's Calendar*, 11th ed. 1806. Reprint, New York: Funk & Wagnalls, 1976.

Meeks, C. J. "Picturesque Eclecticism." *Art Bulletin* 32 (1950): 226–35.

Meyers, Melanie, and Frank Angelo. *An Octagon for the Curriers*. San Francisco: Post Publishing, 1995.

Miles, E. H. "Building a Pergola." *Better Homes and Gardens* 7 (June 1929): 52.

Miller, Angela. *The Empire of the Eye: Landscape Representation and American Cultural Politics*. Ithaca: Cornell University Press, 1993.

Miller, Lillian B., Sidney Hart, and David C. Ward, eds. *The Selected Papers of Charles Willson Peale and His Family*, vol. 2. New Haven: Yale University Press, 1988.

Montgomery, Florence M. *Printed Textiles: English and American Cottons and Linens 1700–1850*. New York: Viking, 1970.

Moore, Ken. "Gazing Globes." *Fine Gardening* 4 (January–February 1992): 30–33.

Morley, John. *Regency Design: Gardens, Buildings, Interiors, Furniture*. New York: Harry N. Abrams, 1993.

"Nature and the Rich." *Garden and Forest* 7 (June 27, 1894): 251–52.

Newberry, Diane. "Charles Willson Peale and His Garden at Belfield." *Journal of New England Garden History* 4 (Spring 1996): 38–47.

Newcomb, Rexford. *Old Kentucky Architecture*. New York: William Helburn, 1940.

Newton, Roger Hale. *Town and Davis Architects: Pioneers in American Revivalist Architecture 1812–70*. New York: Columbia University Press, 1942.

Nicholas, Frederick Doveton and Ralph E. Griswold. *Thomas Jefferson Landscape Architect*. Charlottesville: University Press of Virginia, 1977.

Noble, David W. *The Eternal Adam and the New World Garden*. New York: George Braziller, 1968.

Northend, Mary H. "Practical Pergolas." *House and Garden* 13 (April 1908): 112–16.

———. *Garden Ornaments*. New York: Duffield, 1916.

———. *Remodeled Farmhouses*. Boston: Little, Brown and Company, 1915.

Novotny, Ann. *Alice's World*. Old Greenwich, Conn.: Chatham Press, 1976.

Nygren, Edward J., et al. *Views and Visions: American Landscapes Before 1830*. Washington, D.C.: Corcoran Gallery of Art, 1986.

O'Brien, Raymond J. *American Sublime: Landscape Scenery of the Lower Hudson Valley*. New York: Columbia University Press, 1981.

O'Day, James Robert. "The Colonial Pleasure Garden." *Old-House Journal* 23 (May–June 1995): 26–28.

Olmsted, Frederick Law. *The Cotton Kingdom: A Traveller's Observations on Cotton and Slavery in the American Slave States*. Arthur Schlesinger, ed. New York: Alfred A. Knopf, 1953.

O'Mally, Therese. "Charles Willson Peale's Belfield." *New Perspectives on Charles Willson Peale*. Lillian B. Miller and David C. Ward, eds. Pittsburgh: University of Pittsburgh Press, 1991.

Ortloff, H. Stuart, and Henry B. Raymore. *New Gardens for Old: How To Remodel The Home Grounds*. Garden City, New York: Doubleday, Doran, 1934.

Paine, Albert Bigelow. *Mark Twain: A Biography*. New York: Harper and Brothers, 1922.

Peck, Amelia, ed. *Alexander Jackson Davis: American Architect 1803–1892*. New York: The Metropolitan Museum of Art, 1992.

"Pergolas: The Most Picturesque and Practical Feature of the Modern Outdoor Life." *Craftsman* 20 (September 1911): 575–80.

Perkins, Charlene. "The Gardens at Roseland Cottage." *Early American Life* 12 (June 1991): 48–53.

Peterson, Merrill D., ed. *The Portable Thomas Jefferson*. New York: Viking Penguin, 1977.

Pierson, William H., Jr. *American Buildings and Their Architects: Technology and the Picturesque*. New York: Doubleday, 1978.

Pinkney, Elise, ed. *The Letterbook of Eliza Lucas Pinckney 1739–1762*. Chapel Hill: University of North Carolina Press, 1972.

"Plan of a Garden." *Cultivator* 8 (1851): 22.

Poesch, Jessie. "Germantown Landscapes: A Peale Family Amusement." *Antiques* 73 (November 1957): 434–39.

Polasek, Emily M. K. *A Bohemian Girl in America*. Rollins, Fla.: Rollins Press, 1982.

Powell, Edward Payson. *The Country Home*. New York: McClure Phillips, 1904.

Price, Susan Davis. *Minnesota Gardens, an Illustrated History*. Afton, Minn.: Afton Historical Society Press, 1995.

Prideaux, Gwynn Cochran. *Summerhouses of Virginia*. Richmond: The William Byrd Press, 1976.

Priestman, Mabel Tuke. *Artistic Homes*. Chicago: A. C. McClurg, 1910.

Punch, Walter T., ed. *Keeping Eden: A History of Gardening in America*. Boston: Little, Brown, 1992.

Rauschenberg, Bradford L. "An American Eighteenth-Century Garden Seat." *The Luminary* 18 (Spring 1997): 3–5, 8.

Raymore, Henry B. "On the Way from Here to There: Gates and Entrances." *Home Garden* 4 (July 1944): 48–52.

Reed, James. *Sir Walter Scott: Landscape and Locality*. London: The Attlone Press, 1980.

Richards, T. Addison. "Idlewild—the Home of N. P. Willis." *Harper's New Monthly Magazine* 16 (January 1858): 145–66.

———. "Sunnyside," *Harper's New Monthly Magazine*. 14 (December 1856): 1–21.

Richardson, Edgar P., Brooke Hindle, and Lillian B. Miller. *Charles Willson Peale and His World*. New York: Harry N. Abrams, 1982.

Robinson, Philip L. "The Social Garden Area." *The Home Garden* 16 (December 1950): 25–29.

Rogers, George C., Jr. "Gardens and Landscapes in Eighteenth Century South Carolina." *Eighteenth Century Life* 8 (January 1983): 148–58.

Rogers, W. S. *Garden Planning*. Garden City, N.J.: Doubleday, Page, 1911.

Rorschach, Kimberly. *The Early Georgian Landscape Garden*. New Haven: Yale Center for British Art, 1983.

"The Rustic Touch in the Garden." *The Ladies' Home Journal* 19 (May 1901): 23.

"Rustic Work for the Lawn." *American Gardening* 16 (February 23, 1895): 75.

Sale, Edith Tunis, ed. *Historic Gardens of Virginia*. Richmond: James River Garden Club, 1923.

"Salem: Its Houses, Its Streets and Its Gardens Rich With the Atmosphere of Romance and Tradition." *Craftsman* 25 (October 1913): 36–45.

Sargent, Charles Sprague. "Formal Gardening: Does it Conflict with the Natural Style?" *Garden and Forest* 6 (March 5, 1895): 119–20.

———. "Formal Gardening: When It Can Be Used To Advantage." *Garden and Forest* 6 (March 22, 1893): 129–30.

Sarudy, Barbara Wells. "A Chesapeake Craftsman's Eighteenth-Century Gardens." *Journal of Garden History* 9 (1989): 141–52.

———. "A late eighteenth-century 'tour' of Baltimore gardens." *Journal of Garden History* 9 (1989): 125–40.

Schroer, Mary. "Prairie Gothic." *Fine Gardening* 8 (March–April 1996): 62–67.

Schuyler, David. *Apostle of Taste: Andrew Jackson Downing, 1815–1852*. Baltimore: Johns Hopkins University Press, 1996.

Scott, Frank Jesup. *The Art of Beautifying Suburban Home Grounds*. New York: D. Appleton, 1870.

Seeber, Barbara H. "An Orderly Retreat." *Garden Design* 16 (April–May 1996): 124–27.

Shackleton, Robert and Elizabeth. *Adventures in Home Making*. New York: John Lane, 1910.

Sheaff, Katherine (Mrs. George). Diaries 1838–1850. Fort Washington, Penn., The Highlands Historical Society.

Shelton, Louise. *Beautiful Gardens in America*. New York: Charles Scribner's Sons, 1915.

"The Simple Rural Cottage." *The Horticulturist* 1 (September 1846): 107–10.

Smith, Benjamin. "Letters from William Hamilton to his Private Secretary." *Pennsylvania Magazine of History and Biography* 29 (January 1905): 70–78.

Smith, Charles H. *Landscape Gardening: Or Parks and Pleasure Grounds*. New York: C. M. Saxton, 1856.

Smith, Helen Evertson. "An Ancient Garden." *Century Magazine* 72 (May 1906): 112–19.

Smith, Sarah Bixby. *Adobe Days*. Lincoln: University of Nebraska Press, 1987.

Smithsonian Institution. Archives of American Gardens. Washington, D.C.

Smithsonian Institution. Historic American Buildings Survey Archives. Washington, D. C.

Snyder, H. Rossiter. "The garden living room." *The American Home* 3 (May 1929): 173–74.

"Some Remarks on the Landscape Art." *Bulletin of the American Art Union* 2 (December 1849): 18.

Spencer, Darrell. *The Gardens of Salem*. Winston-Salem, N.C.: Old Salem, 1997.

Spivy, Mary Plant. "Gardens in Nineteenth Century Deerfield; a Rabbit's Eye View of the Street." Typescript. Deerfield, Massachusetts: Historic Deerfield Fellows Program, 1975.

Stand-Tucci, Douglass. *Built in Boston: City and Suburb 1800–1950*. Amherst: University of Massachusetts, 1978.

Starr, Kevin. *Americans and the California Dream 1850–1915*. New York: Oxford University Press, 1973.

Stein, Susan. *The Worlds of Thomas Jefferson at Monticello*. New York: Harry N. Abrams, 1993.

Stilgoe, John R. *Borderland: Origins of the American Suburb, 1820–1939*. New Haven: Yale University Press, 1988.

———. *Common Landscape of America, 1580 to 1845*. New Haven: Yale University Press, 1982.

Sutton, Robert K. *Americans Interpret the Parthenon*. Niwot, Colo.:

University Press of Colorado, 1992.

Swasey, W. F. *Early Days and Men of California*. Oakland: Pacific Press, 1891.

Sweeting, Adam. *Reading Houses and Building Books*. Hanover, N.H.: University Press of New England, 1996.

Tabor, Grace. "An adaptable gated arbor." *The American Home* 4 (March 1930): 576.

Tatum, George B., and Elisabeth Blair MacDougall, eds. *Prophet with Honor: The Career of Andrew Jackson Downing 1815–1852*. Washington, D.C.: Dumbarton Oaks, 1989.

Thomason, Julia H. "Fabulous Finds for the Garden." *Southern Living* 29 (February 1994): 94.

Thompson, Adaline. "A Woman's Two-Year-Old Hardy Garden from Seed." *American Homes and Gardens* 8 (March 1911): 95–96.

Thornton, Tamara Platkins. *Cultivating Gentlemen: The Meaning of Country Life among the Boston Elite 1785–1860*. New Haven: Yale University Press, 1989.

Thorpe, Patricia. "Planting Between the Lines." *House and Garden* (August 1990): 122–26, 151.

Toole, Robert M. "An American Cottage Ornee: Washington Irving's Sunnyside." *Journal of Garden History* 12 (January–March 1992): 52–72.

Trostel, Michael T. "The Maryland Orangeries." *Magnolia* 12 (Spring/Summer 1996): 1–6.

Tunnard, Christopher. "The Romantic Suburb in America." *Magazine of Art* 40 (May 1947): 184–87.

Tyler, Ron. *Visions of America: Pioneer Artists in a New Land*. New York: Thames and Hudson, 1983.

"Ugly Homes and Bad Morals."*Artsman* 3 (December 1905): 73–78.

Underwood, Loring. *The Garden and Its Accessories*. Boston: Little, Brown, 1907.

Upton, Dell. "Pattern-Books and Professionalism, Aspects of the Transformation of Domestic Architecture in America 1800–1860." *Winterthur Portfolio* 19 (Summer/Autumn 1984): 107–50.

———, ed. *Common Places: Readings in American Vernacular Architecture*. Athens, Ga.: University of Georgia Press, 1986.

"The Use of Ornaments in Landscape Gardening." *The Horticulturist* 9 (August 1864): 246.

"A Visit to Montgomery Place." *The Horticulturist* 2 (July 1847): 153–60.

Vivian, J. "Rustic Furniture Adirondack Style." *Mother Earth News* 24 (December–January 1995): 30–39, 96–98.

Vlach, John Michael. *Back of the Big House: The Architecture of Plantation Slavery*. Chapel Hill: University of North Carolina Press, 1993.

Vogel, Penny. "A Design from the Heart." *Fine Gardening* 6 (July–August 1993): 58–61.

Wagner, Charles. *The Simple Life*. Translated by Mary Louise Hendee. New York: McClure, Phillips, 1904.

Walker, Peter. "The Practice of Landscape Architecture in the Postwar United States." Marc Treib, ed. *Modern Landscape Architecture*. Cambridge, Mass.: M.I.T. Press, 1993.

Watkin, David. *The English Vision: The Picturesque in Architecture, Landscape and Garden Design*. New York: Harper and Row, 1982.

Waugh, Frank. *Book of Landscape Gardening: Treatise on the General Principles Governing Outdoor Art*. New York: Orange Judd, 1926.

Weber, Susan Bartlett. *Justin Smith Morrill Homestead*. Montpelier, Vt.: Division for Historic Preservation, 1993.

Weitze, Karen G. *California's Mission Revival*. Los Angeles: Hennessy and Ingalls, 1984.

Wheeler, Candace. *Household Art*. New York: Harper, 1893.

Wheelwright, Robert. *Colonial Gardens: The Landscape Architecture of George Washington's Time*. Washington, D. C.: Institute of Landscape Architects, 1982.

Whitaker, Barbara. "Why Those Backyards Are Looking Like Versailles." *The New York Times* (June 23, 1966): sections 3, 9.

Whiteson, Leon. *A Garden Story*. San Francisco: Mercury House, 1995.

Whitney, The Rev. Peter. *The History of the County of Worcester*. Worcester, Mass.: Isaiah Thomas, 1793.

Wilder, Louise Beebe. *Colour in My Garden*. 1918. Reprint, New York: Atlantic Monthly Press, 1990.

———. *My Garden*. New York: Doubleday, Page, 1916.

Williams, George Alfred. "New England Gardens." *Ladies Home Journal* 41 (May 1924): 165.

Willis, N. P. *Out-doors at Idlewild or the Shaping of a Home on Banks of the Hudson*. New York: Charles Scribner, 1855.

Wisbe, Robert H. *The Search For Order 1877–1920*. New York: Hill and Wang, 1967.

Wolfe, Tom. *From Bauhaus to Our House*. New York: Farrar, Straus & Giroux, 1981.

Woods, May, and Arete Warren. *Glass Houses*. London: Aurum Press, 1988.

Wright, Gwendolyn. *Building the Dream: A Social History of Housing in America*. New York: Pantheon, 1981.

Wright, Richardson. *The Winter Diversions of a Gardener*. Philadelphia: J. B. Lippincott Co., 1934.

Zetlin, Minda. "A 19th-Century Romance." *Nation's Business* 84 (December 1996): 13–14.

INDEX

Pages in *italics* refer to captions and illustrations

ACKNOWLEDGMENTS

This book came about as a result of my efforts to understand the social and stylistic contexts of the wooden structures that have decorated American gardens since colonial times. That I had the temerity to even attempt such a task reveals how imperfect was my knowledge of architectural and garden history. I am now beginning to know what I don't know, and am indebted to the many historians of both architecture and gardens cited in the bibliography.

Scores of colleagues offered fruitful suggestions and shared unpublished research; their help and encouragement was invaluable. The generosity of historical societies, museums, art galleries, many private collectors, and gardeners across the country made possible the illustrations of American paintings and period photographs that enliven this brief history for me, and, I hope, for the reader.

The creation of a fine illustrated book from an imperfect text and a collection of photographs is a daunting task. For accomplishing it so brilliantly, while enduring my vagaries of spelling and method, I owe tremendous thanks to my editor, Ruth Peltason, and to the designer, Ana Rogers. Finally, I would like to thank Rachel Pachter for her help with the morass of correspondence and bibliography, my family for their unfailing support, and my agent, Helen Pratt, for always being there.

MAY BRAWLEY HILL
New York City

PHOTOGRAPH CREDITS

The author and publisher wish to thank the individuals, galleries, and institutions for permitting the reproduction of works in their collections. Those credits not listed in the captions are provided below. All references are to page numbers.

Antiques Collaborative, Inc., Quechee, Vermont: 114; Courtesy Berry-Hill Galleries: 74; Photograph by D. DeCesare: 128; Photograph by James Dee: 135; Department of Library Services (neg. 245330): 89 (above); Lois Dodd: 130; Joellyn Duesberry: 131; Edward Giobbi: 126; James and Nancy Glazer Antiques: 84; Godel and Company Fine Arts, New York: 2–3; James Graham & Sons: 83; Dale and Ann Knight Gutman: 133; Marie's Hollow Herb Farm, Vienna, Missouri: 137; Photograph by Kay Craine Martin: 116; Photograph by Kent Murray: 129; Photograph by Sally Piland: 79; Dean Riddle: 138; Romancing the Woods, Woodstock, New York: 134 (below); Barbara Wells Sarudy: 12 (below); Spanierman Gallery, New York: 101, 105; Dr. and Mrs. Richard Studebaker: 134 (above); David Wheatcroft Antiques: 78.